CONFESSIONS OF THE CZARINA

First published 1918
This edition published by Lector House in 2024

ISBN: 978-93-6138-405-9

Lector House LLP
Registered Office: H. No. 96, Block C, Tomar Colony,
Burari, Delhi – 110084, India
info@lectorhouse.com
www.lectorhouse.com

CONFESSIONS OF THE CZARINA

COUNT PAUL-VASSILI (CATHERINE RADZIWILL)

2024

LECTOR HOUSE

LECTOR HOUSE LLP

The Czarina

From a photograph taken shortly before the Czar's downfall.

CONFESSIONS OF THE CZARINA

BY

COUNT PAUL-VASSILI

Author of
"BEHIND THE VEIL AT THE RUSSIAN COURT"
"LA SOCIÉTÉ DE BERLIN"

ILLUSTRATED

PUBLISHERS' NOTE

A FEW months before the great war broke out, there appeared a book, which, under the title *Behind the Veil of the Russian Court,* bearing the signature of Count Paul Vassili, a name that had become famous through the publication of the volume called *La Société de Berlin*. A lively interest was aroused by *Behind the Veil of the Russian Court,* dealing as it did with the intimate existence of four Russian Sovereigns and their respective Courts. The author of this book was declared to be already dead, out of a very natural feeling of precaution for his personal safety. Count Vassili was living in Petrograd at the time, and most certainly would have been banished to Siberia, and perhaps tried for *lèse-majesté,* if that fact had been discovered. At the present moment the reasons for concealing it exist no longer, and Count Vassili is free to live once more and to publish another work of even greater interest—the life of the former Czarina Alexandra. In relating it, together with some most characteristic incidents which so far are but little known, Count Vassili remarks to the public what a small circle only have known; persons more or less interested in keeping the facts as secret as possible. Count Vassili had known the Empress personally, in fact was regularly and most exactly informed by numerous friends as to all that went on at the Russian Court, and with all manner of intimate details concerning the existence led by the Czar and by his Consort in their Palace of Tsarskoye Selo. It is interesting to note that in *Behind the Veil of the Russian Court,* written at a time when but few people foresaw the fall of the dynasty of Romanoff, Count Vassili declared the event bound to take place in the then very near future.

CONTENTS

INTRODUCTION

I AM not a coward, and it was not out of a feeling of uneasiness in regard to my personal safety, that I had not the courage to publish in my own name the book which, some thirty years ago, produced such a sensation when it appeared in the *Nouvelle Revue* of Madame Adam, under the title of "La Société de Berlin." But I was living in Germany at the time, and though I would have felt delighted had the publication of this volume driven me out of the Prussian capital, from which I was to shake the dust from my shoes with such joy, a few years later, I had there relatives who would most undoubtedly have fared very badly at Bismarck's hands, had my identity been disclosed. And once I am alluding to these distant times, it is just as well to say that the book in question had not at first been written for the benefit of the general public, but consisted of private letters addressed to Madame Adam, who, being happily still in the land of the living, can add many corroborative details. She suggested to me to publish some of these letters; I assented without suspecting the scandal which would follow, and which I do not regret in the very least, now that events have justified the mistrust with which the Prussian monster inspired me. The secret was well kept and one of the victims of it was poor Mr. Gérard, the secretary of Queen Augusta, who was accused of being the author of this book, an accusation that has clung to him ever since, and from which I am happy to relieve him.

The success of *La Société de Berlin* induced Madame Adam to publish other letters in the same style, devoted to other European capitals, with which, however, I had nothing to do, except those dealing with St. Petersburg life. The pseudonym of Count Paul Vassili remained a kind of public property divided between the *Nouvelle Revue* and my poor self. Just before the war, when, indignant at the manner in which Nicholas II. was compromising the work of his great father, I wrote the book *Behind the Veil of the Russian Court,* I bethought myself of assuming once more the old pseudonym. I was living at the time in St. Petersburg, as Petrograd was still called, and my brothers were in the Russian military service. I did not wish them to get into trouble. As it happened, my identity was suspected, and unpleasantness followed; but it is no stigma to have been ostracized by the Russian police under the old régime, so I did not mind or care.

I had not written the book out of any motives of revenge; on the contrary, I had many reasons to be personally grateful to Nicholas II. for various kindnesses I had met with at his hands; but it was impossible for any real Russian patriot to gaze unmoved at the German propaganda that was going on in the Empire, or to forgive its Sovereign Lady for disgracing herself together with the crown she wore, by the superstitious practices that had put her into the power of intriguing persons who ultimately brought about her own destruction, together with the ruin of the dynasty. It was impossible for any one who had known Russia during the reign of Alexander III., when the whole of Europe had its eyes turned upon her, and was clamoring for her alliance, not to feel deeply grieved in noticing the signs of the coming catastrophe which had been hovering in the air ever since the fatal Japanese war. The Monarch had become estranged from his people and his wife was the person responsible for it; or rather the people who had succeeded in getting hold of her mind. I do not wish here to throw stones at Alexandra Feodorowna, and in relating now what I know concerning her life, I will try not to forget that misfortune has got claims upon human sympathy, and that where a woman is concerned one is bound to be even more careful than in the case of a man.

The former Empress of All the Russias is to-day a prisoner, condemned to a horrible exile. She deserves indulgence; the more so that her follies, errors, and mistakes were partly due to a morbid state of mind, verging if not achieving actual insanity. Her existence, like that of the hero in the beautiful poem of Félix d'Arvers, had its secrets, and her soul its mysteries. The fact that she was a Sovereign did not shield her from feminine weaknesses, and, though she had always remained an innocent woman—a fact upon which one cannot sufficiently insist—in view of all the calumnies which have been heaped upon her, yet, like the unfortunate Marie Antoinette, to whom she has been more than once compared, she had also met on her path the devotion of a Fersen, as accomplished, as brave, and as handsome, as the Swedish officer whose name has gone down to posterity, thanks to his love for the poor Queen who perished on the scaffold of the Champs Elysées. While the latter was spared the sorrow of losing such a faithful friend, Alexandra Feodorowna was destined to be an unwilling witness of a cruel and unexpected tragedy, which ended brutally any dreams she might have nursed in the secret of her heart, and put her good name at the mercy of an infuriated man. Therein lies the drama of her life; a drama the remembrance of which probably haunts her to this day in the solitude of the lonely Siberian town, to which she has been banished by a triumphant Revolution.

This drama, which I am going to relate in the pages about to follow, was made the subject of a shameless exploitation that took advantage of the sorrow and despair to which it gave rise, that neither spared the woman nor respected the Sovereign, and that finally overthrew the Romanoff dynasty, and brought about the ruin of Russia. It seems to me that the revelation of it can harm neither its heroine, nor the country over which she reigned for twenty-two years; while, on the other hand, it may help the public to understand some of the causes of the great Revolution which was to be followed by such momentous consequences, not only for Russia, but also for the whole world.

Before relating it, I must, however, beg my readers to keep always in mind the fact that the Consort of Nicholas II. was not a normal woman; that madness was hereditary in the Hesse-Darmstadt family to which she belonged, twenty-two members of whom had, during the last hundred years or so, been confined in lunatic asylums; that consequently a different standard of criticism must be applied to Alexandra Feodorowna than to an ordinary person in full possession of all her intellectual faculties. The whole course of her history proves the truth of what I have just said, and claims indulgence for her conduct.

As for this history, I think that, such as it really was, few people have so far come to an exact knowledge of it, and that no one yet has related it as I am going to do. The information that has reached me has come almost day by day from sources which I have every reason to know are excellent. I have applied myself to eliminate many facts which appeared to me to be of too sensational a nature. I want also to point out to the reader that, though this book is called the *Confessions of the Czarina,* yet it does not contain one single word which I would like him to believe to have been uttered personally by the former Czarina. It is a story written ONLY by Count Paul Vassili, who accepts its responsibility in signing his name to it.

PAUL VASSILI.

February, 1918.

CHAPTER I

BETROTHAL AND MARRIAGE

TOWARD the close of February in the year 1894 the health of the Czar Alexander III. of Russia began to fail.

Those in the confidence of the inner circle of the Imperial Family, who constituted the small society which used to form the immediate surroundings of the Sovereign, whispered that the Emperor was taking a long time to rally from the attack of influenza which had prostrated him in the beginning of the winter, and that steps ought to be taken to ascertain whether or not he was suffering from something other than the weakness which generally follows upon this perfidious ailment. But they did not dare to mention openly their fears, because it was the tradition at the Russian Court that the Czar ought not, and could not, be ill; whenever any bulletins were published concerning his health or that of any other member of the Imperial Family, it was immediately accepted by the general public as meaning that the end was approaching. In the case of Alexander III., his robust appearance, gigantic height and strength, seemed to exclude the possibility of sickness ever laying its grip upon him. In reality things were very different. The Czar had been suffering for years from a kidney complaint, which had been allowed to develop itself without anything being done to stop, or at least to arrest, its progress. He was by nature and temperament an indefatigable worker, accustomed to spending the best part of the day and a considerable portion of the night, seated at his writing-desk; he rarely allowed himself any vacations, except during his summer trips to Denmark, and he never complained when he felt unwell, or would admit that his strength was no longer what it had been. He had a most wonderful power of self-control and a very high idea of his duties as a Sovereign. On the day of his accession to the Throne, when, on his entering for the first time the Anitchkoff Palace, which was to remain his residence until his death, he was greeted by the members of his household with the traditional bread and salt, which is always offered in Russia upon occasions of the kind. When implored to show himself a father to his subjects, the giant's blue eyes had shone with even more kindness in their expression than was generally the case, and in a very distinct and quiet voice he had replied:

"Yes, I will try to be always a father to my people."

This promise, given in the solemn moment when the weight of his new duties and responsibilities was laid upon him, the late Czar had always kept faithfully, honestly, with a steadfast purpose and an indomitable will. He had put upon his program among other things the resolution never to complain at any personal ailment or misfortune that he might find himself obliged to bear. This resolution he kept up to the last moment, and he went on working at his daily task until at last the pen fell from his weary fingers and he had to own himself beaten. But during the last memorable year of his life he must have more than once felt that the end was drawing near, though he never spoke about it, with the exception of once, when finding himself alone with one of his intimate friends, General Tcherewine, he told him that he did not think he had long to live, adding, sadly:

"And what will happen to this country when I am no longer here?"

The General became so alarmed at this avowal of a state of things he had suspected, without daring to acknowledge, that he tried to open the eyes of Empress Marie as to the state of health of her husband. But the Czarina refused to see that anything was the matter, and angrily reproved the General for daring to suggest such a thing. The latter subsided, and sought one of the doctors who were generally in attendance on the Emperor, asking him to tell him honestly his opinion concerning the Czar. The doctor retrenched himself behind professional secrecy, and only replied vaguely. The truth of the matter was that he did not wish to own that he had been rebuffed by Alexander III. when he had asked the latter to allow him to make an examination of him, and that he had never dared to insist on its necessity.

At this time, when his father's life was trembling in the balance, the heir to the Russian Throne, the Grand-Duke Cesarewitsch, was twenty-six years old. If the traditions of the House of Romanoff had been adhered to in regard to him, he ought to have been married already, as it had been settled by custom that the eldest son of the Czar ought as early as possible to bring home a bride, so as to insure the succession to the crown. But the Empress Marie had never looked with favor at the possibility of seeing her family circle widened by the advent of a daughter-in-law, and whenever the question of the establishment of her eldest son was raised she always found objections to offer against any princess whose name was mentioned to her as that of a possible wife. The French party at the Imperial Court, which at that moment was in possession of great influence, tried hard to bring about the betrothal of the future Czar with the Princess Hélène of Orléans, and at one time it seemed as if it would be really possible to arrange such a marriage, in spite of the difference of religion.

But another circumstance interfered; during one of his visits to Germany, where he often repaired as the guest of his aunt, the Grand-Duchess Marie Alexandrowna of Coburg, the Grand Duke had fallen in love with the Princess Margaret of Prussia, the youngest daughter of the Empress Frederick, and the sister of William II., and had declared that he would not marry any one else. To this, however, Alexander III. decidedly objected, saying that he would never consent to a Prussian princess wearing again the crown of the Romanoffs. He expressed himself in such positive terms in regard to this matter that the Grand Duke did not dare to push it forward, and it was soon after this that he was sent on a journey round the world, while the Princess Margaret was hurried into a marriage with a Prince of Hesse by her brother, who, furious at her rejection by the Czar, decided to wed her offhand to the first eligible suitor who presented himself. The young girl wept profusely, but had to obey, and the Cesarewitsch for the first time in his life showed some independence, and declared to his friends that since he had not been allowed to marry the woman he loved, he would not marry at all.

Before this, however, there had been made by his aunt, the Grand-Duchess Elisabeth, an attempt to betroth him with the latter's sister, the Princess Alix of Hesse, who had spent a winter season in St. Petersburg as her guest, and who was spoken of as likely to be considered an eligible bride for the future Emperor of All the Russias. She was not yet as beautiful as she was to become later on. The awkwardness of her manners had not impressed favorably St. Petersburg society. Smart women had ridiculed her and made fun of her dresses, all "made in Germany," and had objected to the ungraceful way in which she danced, and declared her to be dull and stupid. If one is to believe all that was said at the time, the Grand-Duke Nicholas Alexandrowitch shared this opinion, and it was related that, one evening during a supper at the mess of the Hussar regiment of which he was captain, he had declared to his comrades that there was as much likelihood of his marrying the Princess Alix as there was of his uniting himself to the Krzesinska, the dancer who for some years already had been his mistress. But during the spring of the year 1894 things had changed. As the Czar's health became indifferent, his Ministers bethought themselves that it was almost a question of state to marry as soon as possible the Heir to the Throne.

Mr. de Giers, who was in possession of the portfolio of Foreign Affairs, and who (this by the way) had always been pro-German in his sympathies, gathered sufficient courage to mention the subject to Alexander III., saying that the nation wished to see the young Grand Duke married and father of a family. The Emperor understood, and a few days later, in despatching his son to Coburg to attend the nuptials of his cousin, the Princess Victoria Mélita, with the Grand Duke of Hesse, he told him that he would like him to ask for the hand of the Princess Alix, and to offer to the latter the diadem of the Romanoffs.

The Cesarewitsch did not object this time. For one thing, he did not think his father was really ill, and he was becoming very impatient at the state of subjection in which he was being kept by his parents. He imagined that, once he was married, he would be free to live his own life; what he had seen of the Princess Alix had not given him a very high opinion of her mental capacities, and therefore he believed that she would be contented with the grandeur that was being put in her way, and would shut her eyes to any little excursions he might make outside the beaten tracks of holy matrimony. The woman he had loved had been removed from his path, and perhaps in the secret of his soul he was not so very sorry, after all, to show her that he had consoled himself. It seems also that Miss Krzesinska, the Polish dancer by whom he had had two sons, had been won over to the marriage by means about which the less said the better, and had used her influence over her lover to persuade him that the Princess Alix was of so meek and mild a temperament that they would be able to continue their relations after his marriage with her, which perhaps would not be the case were he to wed some one gifted with more independence and more intellect. Nicholas has always been of the same opinion as that of the last person with whom he spoke. He therefore yielded, went dutifully to Coburg, and just as dutifully proposed to the young Princess whose arrival in Russia was to herald so much misfortune to her new family, as well as to her new country.

The engagement was announced on the 20th of April, 1894, but was not made in Russia the subject of welcome it had been expected. Everybody felt that love had played no part in this union, which politics alone had inspired. The open repugnance which the bride displayed for everything that was Russian, and the hesitation she had shown before consenting to adopt the orthodox faith, had not predisposed in her favor St. Petersburg society. The Empress Marie, whose consent had been a matter of necessity, did not hide the want of sympathy with which this marriage inspired her; the Imperial Family did not care to see put over its head the insignificant Princess it had snubbed two years before; the nation, violently anti-German as it had become, wondered why it had not been possible to find for its future Sovereign a wife in some other country than the one which seemed to consider as its right the privilege of furnishing Russia with its Empresses.

By a curious anomaly, in Darmstadt, and in Berlin, the betrothal was exceedingly unpopular, and the press spoke of it as of an open scandal, on account of the change of religion imposed upon the Princess Alix. The only two people who rejoiced at her good luck were Queen Victoria, who always liked to see her daughters and granddaughters well married; and the Kaiser, who, since his earliest years, had been the particular friend of the future Czarina, and who had succeeded, at the time when she had shown herself reticent in regard to all her other relatives, in winning her confidence and her affection, perhaps out of gratitude, because he had been the only one who had troubled about her in general.

The first weeks which followed upon the engagement of the Cesarewitsch were spent by him in England, whither his fiancée had repaired, and while there he had been very much impressed with the grandeur of Great Britain, and with the kindness which Queen Victoria showed him. He would have liked nothing better than to be allowed to remain where he was for an indefinite time, forgetting all about Russia, which (this is unfortunately an uncontested fact) he never liked nor troubled about.

Events, however, were progressing, and very soon it became evident even to the most indifferent onlooker that the days of Alexander III. were numbered. The dying Sovereign was taken to Livadia in the Crimea, whither his son was hastily recalled. When the latter arrived there took place a small incident which, better, perhaps, than anything else, will give an idea of the young man's utter want of comprehension of the gravity of the events which went on around him. A few hours after he had reached Livadia his father's friend, General Tcherewine, called upon him, to make him a report concerning the health of the Czar. The Grand Duke listened to him in silence, then suddenly inquired:

"What have you been doing the whole time you have been here? Have you been at the theater, and are there any pretty actresses this year?"

The General, surprised, replied:

"But, Sir, I could not possibly go to the theater while the Emperor is so ill."

"Well, what has this got to do with going or not to the theater; one must spend one's evenings somewhere."

Tcherewine, who related to me himself this story a few weeks later, added:

"He will always remain the same; he will never understand anything that goes on around him."

It was during the last days of the useful life of Alexander III. that the plan of marrying immediately his son and future successor to the Princess Alix of Hesse, and of performing the ceremony at Livadia, was suggested, at the instigation, it is said, of the German Ambassador in St. Petersburg, General von Schweinitz, who had received instructions from Berlin to try and hasten the event as much as possible. But the Czar would not hear of it, declaring that the Heir to the Russian Throne could not be married privately. He consented, however, to a telegram being sent to the Princess Alix, inviting her to come at once to Livadia, to be presented to him. She obeyed the summons, but not without reluctance. She did not care for her future husband, and as she elegantly expressed it, to a lady whom she honored with her confidence, she "did not care to find herself in the Crimea at a time when no one would think of her, and when she would be compelled to be the fifth wheel to a coach." She was, however, persuaded, and left for Warsaw, where her sister, the Grand-Duchess Elisabeth, was to receive her, and to accompany her farther.

At Berlin she was met by William II., who traveled with her a part of the way, and during a long interview which lasted over five hours gave her his instructions as to what she ought to do in the future. As we shall see, she was to follow them but too well.

The Princess reached Livadia three days before the Czar breathed his last. He found sufficient strength to receive her, bless her, and wish her happiness in her new life. She replied (this must be conceded to her) with great tact to those solemn words of farewell, and, suddenly surmounting her previous repugnance, she declared herself ready to abjure at once the Protestant faith, and to embrace that of her future husband and subjects. Some people say that she declared she wished to procure this last joy for Alexander III., but this is doubtful, considering the fact that her conversion took place only on the morrow of the death of the latter.

As soon as it had become an accomplished fact, she was given the title of a Russian Grand Duchess and of an Imperial Highness. Her name appeared in the liturgy, and she was treated with all the honors pertaining to a future Empress. But she found herself lonely and forsaken amid her newly acquired grandeur. The Dowager Empress was too entirely taken up by her grief to pay any attention to the haughty girl, who, already during those first few days of her new life, showed herself resentful when she thought that she was not awarded sufficient importance. The young Czar was so absorbed by the many duties and obligations which fell upon his shoulders that he had no time to remain with her as long as she would have wished, perhaps, and his family simply ignored her. Her days were spent in attending the many funeral services which, according to etiquette, took place twice, and sometimes thrice, daily beside the bier of the deceased Monarch.

She found herself placed not only in an awkward, but also in an absurd, position, and if she did not realize other things, she understood this one but too well.

When the body of Alexander III. was brought back to St. Petersburg, the Princess Alix accompanied it, together with the other members of the Imperial Family, and one could see her, deeply veiled, during the funeral ceremonies which took place at the fortress, standing beside the Dowager Empress, silent and attentive to all that was going on around her, and making mental notes as to everything that was taking place. She began to assume a Sovereign's attitude, and she tried to take, as if accidentally, precedence over the Grand Duchesses. One of them, the Princess Marie Pawlowna, soon perceived the game, and one afternoon as the future bride was keeping close to her prospective mother-in-law, seeming to dance attendance upon the latter, the Grand Duchess pushed her aside most unceremoniously, saying as she did so:

"Not yet, not yet, Alix; this place belongs still to me."

Affronted, the young girl withdrew; but when she got home to the Palace belonging to her sister, where she had taken up her abode, she declared that she wished to return to Darmstadt because her position was too false in Russia.

Scene followed upon scene; and Nicholas II. was treated for the first time to the hysterics of which he was to see, later on, so many repetitions. At last the Prince of Wales, the future Edward VII., interfered, and it was partly at his instigation, and that of Queen Victoria, who wrote upon the subject to the Empress Marie, that it was at last decided that the marriage of the new Czar with the Princess Alix was to take place immediately after the funeral of the former's father.

I shall never forget that day. In the vast halls of the Winter Palace the whole of Russia was represented, eager to witness this unique ceremony, the marriage of a Reigning Emperor, an event which had never taken place before. The bride was on that day the object of great sympathy. One pitied her for finding herself so suddenly placed in a position for which she had not been at all prepared, and one felt disposed to grant her every indulgence in case she made a mistake of some kind or other, which was almost an unavoidable thing. Some people, whose English sympathies predisposed them in her favor, rejoiced openly to see the Throne occupied by a granddaughter of Queen Victoria, and hoped that the latter's influence and example would induce the new Empress to try and persuade her husband to renounce the principles of the tyrannous autocracy followed by his predecessors. The man in the street, however, remarked that nothing but bad omens surrounded this hurried marriage, and recalled the old Russian proverb, that "wedding-bells ought never to be heard in conjunction with funeral ones."

The most unconcerned person seemed to be the bride herself as, amid the hushed expectation of the crowd assembled on her passage, she entered the chapel of the Winter Palace on the arm of him who since a few days was Nicholas II., Emperor and Autocrat of All the Russias.

A murmur of admiration followed her as she passed. Seldom has anything more beautiful graced human eye than Alexandra Feodorowna in her wedding-dress, as she slowly walked along, with a diamond crown on her head and a long mantle of cloth of gold lined with ermine falling from her shoulders, and carried by Court officials in embroidered uniforms. She was a real vision of loveliness, "divinely tall and divinely fair," and in the general feeling of admiration excited by her radiant beauty but few people noticed the thin, set lips, pressed together in firm determination, and the hard chin, which gave a disagreeable expression to what otherwise would have been a faultless face. Behind her, also in white attired, walked the Empress Marie, sobbing the whole time, and leaning on the arm of her aged father, the King of Denmark. Every heart went out to her in her widowhood and loneliness; while many wondered whether her successor, on the Throne she had graced so well, would ever become as popular as she had been during her short reign of thirteen years.

The Czarina

When she was Princess Alix of Hesse-Darmstadt, before her betrothal to the Czar, 1894.

An hour later a State carriage with outriders drove the newly wedded couple from the Winter Palace to that of Anitchkoff where they were to take up their residence with the Dowager Empress until their own apartments were made ready for them. The bride was greeted with vociferous cheers by the crowds. It was the one solitary occasion in her life when she could have the illusion of being popular with her newly acquired subjects. Eighteen months later these were to show to her in an unmistakable manner that such was far from being the case, when she was making her entry into that old town of Moscow, where the Imperial Crown was to be put on her brow, to replace the orange flowers which had adorned her head on her wedding morning.

CHAPTER II

MARRIAGE AND LONELINESS

ONE must be fair. The first months of the wedded life of the young Empress Alexandra were not months of unmixed happiness. This, though partly her fault, was also due to circumstances and the people who surrounded her. Though the Consort of one of the mightiest monarchs in Europe, she yet found herself relegated to an absolutely secondary position; she discovered very quickly that no one considered her to be of any importance whatsoever beside her mother-in-law, the Dowager-Empress Marie. The latter had been one of the most popular Sovereigns who ever graced a throne, and from the very first days after her arrival in Russia she had applied herself to the task of pleasing the people. Like her sister, Queen Alexandra, she identified herself completely with the nation that now claimed her as its own, and she entered into all its interests and pursuits, without any exaggeration, but with that quiet, lovely dignity which never failed her, no matter in what position she found herself. Her influence over her husband had been immense, but no one had ever noticed it; on the contrary, she had persistently remained in the background and tried to pass for a pleasant, amiable, and just a little frivolous, woman who cared for balls, pretty clothes, fine jewels, and the pomp which surrounded her at every step she took. She held very properly the idea that it lowers a Sovereign to appear to be under the sway and influence of his wife, and so, though Alexander III. never took any decision of any importance without having first of all discussed it with her, in public she avoided not only talking politics, but even the appearance of being interested in them.

On the other hand, she had always been, not only conscious, but also very jealous, of her power. She did not in the least care to give it up after her widowhood. Her children, strange to say, had always stood in awe of her, much more than of the Czar, who was a most affectionate and loving father, while Marie Feodorowna had always treated them more from the point of view of Sovereign than mother. This had been especially the case with the Grand-Duke Nicholas, who, when he found himself Emperor, discovered that he could not avoid taking the Dowager Empress's opinion, especially in matters concerning his domestic life. He was told by her that the inexperience of his young wife made it imperative she should be guided by the advices of people older than herself.

This, however, did not suit at all Alexandra Feodorowna, and she found an unexpected support in the person of her own Mistress of the Robes, the Princess Galitzyne, who did not like Marie Feodorowna and was but too glad to put spokes in the latter's wheels. That was the cause of much trouble, and brought about strife in the Imperial Family, which might have been avoided by the exercise of a small amount of tact.

The young Empress, compelled to live in two badly furnished, poky little rooms on the ground floor of the Anitchkoff Palace, became impatient and fretful, and did not care to make a secret of the fact. She felt hurt, too, at several incidents which occurred about that time, the first one of which was connected with the introduction of her name in the liturgy. She wished it to figure immediately after that of the Emperor, while Marie Feodorowna pretended that hers ought not to be relegated to a secondary place, but be mentioned before that of her daughter-in-law.

The two ladies quarreled desperately on this subject, and at last the matter was referred to the Synod, which decided, in view of the existent precedents, that the name of the Consort of the Sovereign ought to be called before that of his mother. The Dowager was furious, while Alexandra Feodorowna was triumphant, and not wise enough to hide it from the world, expressing herself quite loudly in regard to the pleasure which she experienced in seeing defeated the attempt made by her mother-in-law to relegate her to an inferior place which she did not in the least wish to occupy.

Another cause of discontent arose in connection with the Crown Jewels. Marie Feodorowna had liked to wear them more often than any of her predecessors on the Throne, and, though her own private collection of pearls and diamonds was one of the most magnificent in Europe, yet she loved to put on the exceptional stones, tiaras, and necklaces which were the property of the State. Her husband, Czar Alexander III., also liked to see them adorn the person of his idolized wife, and in order to spare her the annoyance of going through the long ceremony associated with the demand of any *parure* it pleased her to require from the Treasury, he had had the jewels she cared for the most transferred to the Anitchkoff Palace, where they were kept in a special safe in the Empress's bedroom. After the latter's widowhood, the question arose as to whether she was to be allowed to retain the custody of all these precious stones, or whether, properly speaking, it was only the reigning Empress who had the right to wear them; had they not better be returned to the place which they had occupied before in the Imperial Treasury?

Some Court officials considered that this was the proper thing to do; the more so that, as it happened, the young Empress had not personal diamonds or pearls at all worthy of her new position. She had received some wonderful presents from her husband when they had become engaged, but the usual amount of jewels bestowed upon marriage on all the Grand Duchesses of Russia had not been offered to her, on account of the hurry with which this marriage had been achieved. It was therefore essential that she should be given the opportunity to adorn herself on all State occasions with the brilliants that the Crown held in reserve for the use of the Sovereign's Consorts. No one thought of subjecting the Empress to the ordeal of going to her mother-in-law, to beg from the latter the permission to use the things to which she was legally entitled, and one would have thought that the best way out of the difficulty would be to have the jewels returned to their original place of abode, and reinstated in the Treasury.

But one had not reckoned with the Dowager Empress! She absolutely refused to give up the ornaments she had been so fond of, and when driven out of her last intrenchments, and obliged to capitulate, she protested that it was not usual for an Empress to wear what belonged to the Crown, before that Crown had been officially laid upon her head, and said that she would relinquish the possession of the famous jewels only after the Coronation of her son and daughter-in-law. The Czar, weak as usual, yielded. Alexandra Feodorowna declared that she did not care for the "hateful things," and proceeded to buy out of her allowance the most gorgeous ornaments she could lay her hands upon, getting heavily into debt in consequence, a fact which did not help to make her popular with her subjects.

She had an unpleasant manner that told against her. Not affable by nature, timid to a certain extent, she imagined that her position as Empress of Russia required her to show herself haughty and disdainful with the people who were introduced to her. Her extremely indifferent knowledge of the French language, which was the only one in use in Court circles, also added to her unpopularity. Her mistakes in that respect were repeated everywhere and ridiculed by the old ladies whom her want of politeness had contributed to offend, and before she had been married three months she found herself not only unpopular, but even disliked by almost every person she had met.

Then, again, Alexandra Feodorowna was possessed of a wonderful, but most unfortunate talent for drawing caricatures, of which she made no secret, but which, on the contrary, used against all those she disliked, and their name was legion! She found herself, of course, extremely lonely, without any friends of her own rank, and deprived of that liberty of going about she had enjoyed so much at Darmstadt. She had taken a violent dislike for all the Princesses belonging to her new family, and even the grace and liveliness of the Grand-Duchess Xenia Alexandrowna, her sister-in-law, had failed to win her heart. She did not care for Russia; its climate did not agree with her, its language she could not learn; its religion she despised in those early days which followed upon her marriage, though she was later to become a fanatical adherent of the Greek Orthodox Church; its manners and customs she could not assimilate. All these circumstances put together made her sullen and angry, and added to her general discontent. She at last determined to try and assert herself, and, though secretly despising the weakness of character of her husband, whom she continually chaffed for his blind submission to his mother, she endeavored to supplant the latter in his heart and mind, and to substitute herself for Marie Feodorowna, not only in domestic, but also in political matters.

We shall presently see how this experiment was to be tried, and what were its ultimate consequences.

CHAPTER III

MY COUNTRY, MY BELOVED COUNTRY, WHY AM I PARTED FROM THEE?

THE spring of 1895 brought few changes in the existence of the young Empress. For one thing, she contrived to influence the Czar to take up his residence in the small Palace of Tsarskoye Selo, which later on they were to inhabit permanently, but which at that time was still badly furnished and rather forlorn in appearance, owing to the fact that no one had ever lived there since the death of Alexander II. It had been a favorite resort of his, and of his morganatic wife, the Princess Youriewsky, and for that reason had been shunned by his successor, who had elected to establish himself in the huge castle of Gatschina. This place was left to the Dowager Empress for life, and thither she repaired in the beginning of the spring, not, however, without having made a feeble attempt to influence her son and daughter-in-law to accompany her. But for once Nicholas II. did not react, and ignored the invitation. His wife was expecting the birth of her first child, and this circumstance gave her more influence, and to her wishes more weight, than would perhaps have been the case under ordinary circumstances.

Though at Tsarskoye Selo Alexandra Feodorowna obtained more liberty than had been the case throughout the weary months of the preceding winter, yet she found that she had to keep in mind the necessity not to give any reason for the criticisms which she knew but too well were directed against her from every side. Needless to say, she might have avoided these criticisms by the display of some elementary notions of tact. In her way she was a very truthful woman; she even carried her love for veracity sometimes too far. She had no experience of the world, and her life at Darmstadt had not prepared her for the responsibilities of her position as Empress. She did not care for St. Petersburg society, which she considered frivolous, and she made no secret of this fact. Of course people resented it.

Her mother-in-law, the Empress Marie, though she had always kept herself very well informed as to all that was going on in the select circles of those privileged beings who were received at Court, yet had taken good care to appear to ignore the many love-affairs which were either known or suspected in regard to these people. She had so much tact that whenever anything she disapproved of occurred, among these Upper Ten Thousand of people, she let them see that such was the case, but never mentioned it in public.

The Empress Alexandra, on the contrary, spoke with acerbity of every small incident which came to her knowledge, and declared loudly that she would refuse to admit in her presence the persons guilty of indiscretions. During the second season which followed upon her marriage, when Court receptions interrupted by the mourning for the late Czar were once more resumed, the Empress struck off from the list of invitations submitted to her the names of some of the most prominent members of St. Petersburg society, giving her reasons for doing so. The result was that nothing but old frumps, or mothers with marriageable daughters, attended this particular ball, and that the Empress in her turn was boycotted by almost everybody of note in the capital, who did not care to have themselves or their relatives publicly branded as not worthy to be admitted within the gates of the Winter Palace. The effects of this ostracism became apparent on the New-Year's reception which followed upon this incident, which only four women attended, wives of Ministers, who, in virtue of their husbands' position, could not well do anything else. The Emperor, surprised at this absence of the feminine element, on an occasion when it was generally very conspicuous, inquired into the matter. When told the story which had given rise to it he forthwith consulted his mother, and the latter, profiting by the occasion, told her son that he had better have the names of the people about to be invited at Court balls submitted to her for inspection, and not to the young Empress. Of course this became known at once, with the result that the popularity of Marie Feodorowna increased, while that of her daughter-in-law, on the contrary, diminished with every day that passed.

Rebuffed on every side, Alexandra Feodorowna first sought comfort and advice from her sister, the Grand-Duchess Elisabeth, who, by reason of her residing in Moscow, where her husband, the Grand-Duke Sergius, occupied the position of Governor-General, did not often see her. The Grand Duchess, in response to an invitation which she received to come to Tsarskoye Selo, took the first train. When consulted by the Empress in regard to the difficulties with which she found her path beset, she could not find a solution for them, perhaps because she did not honestly seek it. Elisabeth, as well as her husband, was very ambitious, and they would not have been sorry to see Alexandra Feodorowna estranged from all her new family, in order to have her entirely under their influence and control, and to dominate through her the weak Nicholas II., whose character was already beginning to be known, with all its faults and defects, by his near relatives, as well as by his Ministers and advisers. Elisabeth, therefore, advised her sister to try and keep at arm's-length from her mother-in-law, uncles, aunts, and cousins, and especially to be suspicious of her two brothers-in-law, who were represented to her as being her natural enemies, notwithstanding the fact that one of them, the Grand-Duke George, was consumptive and did not live in St. Petersburg, the climate of which he could not endure, while the second, the Grand-Duke Michael, was a youth of sixteen, hardly out of school.

Alexandra Feodorowna, however, became suspicious of this advice, perhaps because she distrusted the Grand-Duke Sergius just as much as her other relatives. Yet advice she felt she must have. It would have been natural for her to seek that of her brother, the Grand Duke of Hesse, and of her other sisters, the Princess Victoria of Battenberg and the Princess Henry of Prussia, but while the former had never been her favorite, the latter refused—at the instigation of her husband, most probably—to be mixed up in things which did not concern her, and intrenched herself behind her ignorance of Russian customs and Russian society. The Empress felt frantic, and it was then that she was seized with violent attacks of homesickness, which she did not attempt to conceal. More than once she was heard to say that she wished she were back in Germany, where at least she would find people capable of understanding her and of advising her well and soundly.

Germany has always, as is but too well known to-day, maintained an army of spies in Russia. Very quickly a report of what was going on in Tsarskoye Selo reached the ears of William II. He saw his opportunity and forthwith wrote to his cousin, reminding her of their former friendship and telling her that he was entirely at her disposal to help her, by his knowledge of Russian affairs, which he professed was very great, and by his experience of the world.

The Empress caught at the opportunity, and from that day there was established between them relations of the closest intimacy, linking the Empress and the Lord of Potsdam. She took the habit of sending him a kind of diary of what she was doing and of what went on at the Russian Court—a diary in which she did not spare her mother-in-law, or her husband, whom she reproached with not taking her part more openly.

Of course it was not easy to carry on such a correspondence. The young Empress was closely watched, a fact of which she was but too well aware. She tried the medium of the German Embassy, but apart from the fact that it would have seemed a suspicious thing to send there letters in a regular way, the Ambassador, Prince Radolin, refused to be the means of forwarding messages of which he did not know the import, and did not care to be involved in an intrigue that would inevitably have brought him to grief if discovered. Some other way, therefore, had to be devised, and for a time it seemed as if it would be next to impossible to find any. Once or twice the Princess Hohenlohe, wife of the Imperial Chancellor, who, through the fact that she was the owner of large estates in Lithuania, often visited St. Petersburg, brought with her messages from the Kaiser to the Empress Alexandra, and took back with her to Berlin the latter's replies. But this was not sufficient, and during the first visit paid by the Czar and his Consort to the German Court William and the young Czarina came to an understanding, after which their correspondence continued through the medium of friends of the Kaiser, who somehow appeared regularly in Russia whenever this was considered necessary.

People, and there were some, who happened to be in the secret of this intercourse pretended that one of the things which William II. urged upon his cousin was the necessity of getting rid of the influence of the Empress Marie, who, by reason of her avowed French sympathies, constituted a danger to German expansion and to German progress in the Muscovite Empire. The fact that for the present Alexandra Feodorowna was still considered a nonentity at the Russian Court was not of much importance because it was thought that if she were once to become the mother of a son she would immediately be raised to the position of an important personage in her husband's house and country. And it must not be forgotten that in the course of the summer of 1895 the Empress was known to be about to give birth to her first child, who of course had to be a boy and an Heir to the Russian

Throne.

Alas, alas for these hopes!

It was a Grand Duchess, Olga Nicholaiewna, who saw the light of day on a November morning in the Imperial Palace of Tsarskoye Selo. The disappointment was intense and extended to all classes of the nation, except among the members of the Imperial Family, who made no secret of the fact that they were delighted the little Hessian Princess they all disliked so intensely had not fulfilled her husband's and her subjects' expectations. The news of their joy reached the ears of Alexandra Feodorowna through the channel of the Kaiser, and added to her bitterness against her Russian relatives, which made itself felt in the affected manner with which she continually made allusions in their presence to her regrets at having accepted the position of Empress of All the Russias. She openly spoke of her contempt for this "land of savages" as she called it, and more than once her attendants heard her give vent to the exclamation of "My country, my beloved country, why am I parted from Thee?"

CHAPTER IV

A SAD CORONATION

CONTRARY to the custom observed at the Imperial Court of Russia, the young Empress insisted herself on nursing her baby. This met with general disapproval, not only from Marie Feodorowna, who, never having thought of the possibility of such an infraction of the traditions of the House of Romanoff, felt considerably affronted at this piece of independence on the part of her daughter-in-law; also from all the dowagers of St. Petersburg, who considered the innovation as *infra dig.* and declared that such a breach of etiquette constituted a public scandal.

Some enterprising ladies, who, by virtue of their own unimpeachable positions, thought themselves entitled to express their opinions, ventured to say so to Alexandra Feodorowna herself. She was indignant at what she termed an insult, turned her back on those voluntary advisers, and flatly declared that she would refuse henceforward to admit into her presence people who had forgotten to such an extent the respect due to her and to her position as the wife of their Sovereign.

Matters assumed an acute form, and during the first ball which took place that season in the Winter Palace the incident was discussed most vehemently. One wondered what would happen later on, and how the Empress would behave in regard to those givers of unsought advice in the future. But Providence interfered in favor of Alexandra Feodorowna, because she suddenly was taken with an attack of the measles, not the German ones this time, but the real, authentic thing, and the Court festivities about to take place were immediately postponed in spite of the protestations of different Court officials, who urged that they could very well take place in the absence of the Empress, and that their abandonment would be a serious blow to trade, which already was very bad, and which had discounted the profits it generally made during a winter season when the gates of the Winter Palace were thrown open with the usual lavishness and luxury displayed there on such occasions. Trade and its requirements were about the last thing which troubled the mind of Alexandra Feodorowna. She was of the opinion prevalent in Poland at the time of the Saxon dynasty that when Augustus was intoxicated the whole nation had to get drunk, and though she detested or pretended she detested Court balls and festivities, yet she was adverse to others enjoying them while she herself was debarred from doing so. Girls in their first season eager for showing off their pretty frocks, and lively young married women in quest of gaiety, were told to forego expectations of such pleasure, and the gates of the Palace remained closed for the first time in many years, to the general disappointment of St. Petersburg society and of its prominent members.

This disappointment, however, was soon forgotten in the expectation of the Coronation about to take place, the date of which had been fixed for the 15th of May. Great preparations were made for it. Those who remembered the pomp which had attended that of Alexander III., thirteen years before, wondered whether the ceremony about to be repeated would be as brilliant as the one which they had not yet forgotten. The whole of St. Petersburg society, with few exceptions, repaired to Moscow for the solemn occasion, and all the Foreign Courts sent representatives to attend the festival. One tried to guess how the young Empress would carry herself through the trying ordeal, and whether she would condescend for once to show herself amiable toward her subjects in the ancient capital of Muscovy, the population of which had always professed far more independence of opinions than that of St. Petersburg, where conversations were more restrained and guarded, in view of the constant presence of the Imperial Family within its walls. The one thing which everybody was looking forward to was the public entry of the young Sovereigns in the old town, an entry which was to be made with unusual pomp and solemnity.

I remember very well the day of the ceremony. I had a seat in a house situated on the great square opposite the residence of the Governor-General of the town, a position which was still occupied by the Grand-Duke Sergius. Together with some friends, we watched the long line of troops, followed by representatives from all classes in the country; by Court officials on horseback, in gold-embroidered uniforms, behind whom rode, surrounded by a brilliant staff, the Czar himself, mounted on a gray charger; a small, slight figure, contrasting vividly with his father thirteen years before. Nicholas II. had already acquired the expression of utter impassibility which was never to change in the future. He surveyed with a grim look the vast crowds massed in the streets, who cheered him vociferously, but he did so with a look that expressed neither pleasure nor disappointment, but simply indifference mixed with tediousness.

Behind him came a long row of State carriages all gold and precious stones, the diamonds which glittered on them being valued at several millions of rubles. In the foremost, the carriage of Catherine the Great, with an immense Imperial Crown on its top, rode the Dowager Empress dressed in white and looking as young almost as she had done on the day of her own Coronation. Hurrahs without end greeted her appearance; the people cheered her with an enthusiasm such as had rarely been seen in Russia, while, pale and trembling, she bowed incessantly from right to left, with tears streaming down her cheeks. These hurrahs followed her all along her way from the distant Petrowsky Palace to the gates of the Kremlin, which she entered at last, amid the acclamations of the multitude assembled to see her pass.

Immediately behind her, divided only by a squadron of cavalry, drove her daughter-in-law, also dressed in a white gown, and sparkling with all the jewels belonging to the Crown, which she had assumed for the first time on that solemn day. A dead silence, contrasting painfully with the frenzied reception awarded to Marie Feodorowna, greeted her successor on the Throne of Russia. This contrast was so evident that everybody present was struck with it, and something like a presentiment of evil passed through the mind of most of the assistants of this strange scene. One remembered Marie Antoinette at Rheims during the Coronation of Louis XVI. when she also had been received with silence and contempt by the French nation, who a few years later was to send her to the scaffold.

The Dowager Empress Marie Feodorowna

Perhaps something of the kind crossed the mind of Alexandra Feodorowna herself, because it was evident that she was suffering from a violent desire to give vent to tears and rage. I saw her from the place where I stood, through the open large windows of the State carriage in which she sat quite alone, according to the requirements of etiquette, immovable like an Indian goddess, looking neither right nor left, but straight before her, her haughty head thrown back, two red spots on her cheeks, and a set expression on her thin lips closely joined together. She understood but too well the meaning of this strange reception she was awarded; too proud to complain, she seemed to ignore it. Once and once only did I see her start, and that was when, amid the profound silence which prevailed around her, a voice, that of a child, was heard exclaiming:

"Show me the German, mamma, show me the German!"

And with this cry in her ears and in those of other listeners, the big coach with Alexandra Feodorowna sitting in it, in all the splendor of her white dress and glorious jewels, vanished in the distance within the walls of that old fortress called the Kremlin, which, seen in the glamour of dusk already falling, looked more like a prison than a palace.

Three days later I was to look once more on the slight and erect figure of the Consort of Nicholas II. as she emerged out of the bronze gates of the Cathedral of the Assumption walking under a canopy of cloth of gold and ermine, with ostrich plumes towering on its top, the Crown of the Russian Empresses standing high upon her small head and the long mantle of brocade embroidered with the black eagles of the Romanoffs trailing from her shoulders. She looked magnificent, but there was something in the expression of her haughty features which reminded one of the prophecy of the Italian sculptor in regard to Charles Stuart: "Something evil will befall that man; he has got misfortune written on his face."

Beside his wife, Nicholas II. looked the insignificant personage he was to remain until the end of his reign and very probably of his life. He could no more bear the weight of his Crown physically than he was able later on to carry the burden of his responsibilities. As he walked, he staggered and trembled; and one could distinctly notice the signs of the extreme fatigue under which he labored. Supported on either side by two attendants, who carried the folds of his Imperial mantle, he tried to keep erect the scepter which he held in his right hand, and the orb which reposed in his left.

And then occurred the memorable incident of that memorable day.

When the long procession reached the doors of the Cathedral of the Archangels where, according to custom, the newly crowned Czar was obliged to repair for a short service of thanksgiving, I saw Nicholas II. reel from right to left as would have done a drunken man, and suddenly the scepter which he grasped fell heavily from his hand to the stone floor, before the altar of the church.

It would be difficult to describe the emotion produced by this untoward incident, which was at once interpreted by the superstitious Russian people as a bad omen for the reign which had just begun. Strange though this may seem, yet it is absolutely true, that the faith of the Russian nation in Nicholas II. was shattered from that day when it had found him unable to carry the symbol of his supreme power and Imperial might and not strong enough to bear its weight.

This was not, however, the only unlucky incident which was connected with this sad Coronation, which in so many respects reminded one of several others that had marked the marriage festivities of Marie Antoinette, and the anointing of Louis XVI. at Rheims. I will not describe here the horrors which were enacted on the Khodinka field, when more than twenty thousand people were crushed to death during a popular festival given in honor of the Czar's assuming the Crown of his ancestors; I shall only mention the part played by Alexandra Feodorowna in the gruesome tragedy. As everybody knows, unfortunately for her reputation in history, she danced the night which followed upon it, at the French Embassy. But what is not so well known is the fact that when she and the Emperor were asked by Count de Montebello, the French Ambassador, whether the ball which they had promised to attend had not better be postponed until the next day, which would have been an easy matter, Alexandra Feodorowna had exclaimed that she could not understand why such a fuss was made because "a few peasants had been victims of an accident likely to happen anywhere," while Nicholas II. had replied that he did not see any necessity to make any alteration in the program which had been officially sanctioned and adopted since a long time.

It was only on the third day following upon the catastrophe, when the clamors of public opinion reached even the deaf ears of the Czar and of his Consort, that they decided themselves at last to pay a visit to the various hospitals where the victims of the tragedy had been carried. They went there in great state and ceremony, the Empress dressed in lace and satin, holding in her hands a large bouquet of flowers which had been presented to her by the officials to whom had been deputed the charge of receiving her at the gates of the houses of suffering and death, whither her duties had called her, much against her will. It was related later on that a little girl ten years old or so, perceiving the roses held by the Sovereign, had exclaimed:

"Oh, the pretty roses!"

"Give them to her," said the Emperor.

"Certainly not. Flowers are most unwholesome in a sick-room," replied Alexandra Feodorowna, and she turned away without another word.

CHAPTER V

DAUGHTERS, DAUGHTERS, AND NO SON

IT was not generally known at the time of the Coronation that the Empress was about to become a mother for the second time. She had not mentioned the fact to her family and not to her mother-in-law, not wishing to be bothered with advice as to the manner in which she should take care of herself—advice which she was beforehand determined not to follow. But the strain of the Coronation festivities, with their attendant emotions and unavoidable fatigue, told upon her, and this was the principal reason which induced the Emperor to repair with her to Illinskoye, the country-seat of the Grand-Duke Sergius, close to Moscow, immediately after the departure of the Foreign Envoys, who had been sent to Russia to represent their respective Governments.

The public wondered at this decision, the more so that it was openly said that the responsibility for the disaster of Khodinka rested with the Grand Duke, who had not known how to take the necessary precautions, which, if resorted to, would have prevented the catastrophe. No one suspected that the real reason for this determination of Nicholas II. to spend a few quiet weeks with his uncle and brother-in-law was due to the state of health of Alexandra Feodorowna.

The measure, however, was not to prove successful, because a very few days after the arrival of the Imperial pair at Illinskoye its hopes of an increase in the family were dashed to the ground, and an unlucky accident deprived the Empress of a son and the country of an heir, it having been proved that the child born too early was of the male sex. The fact was kept a close secret, as those in authority did not care for the nation to become aware of the disappointment which had overtaken its Monarch, and even Alexandra Feodorowna was not told of the full extent of the misfortune. She learned of it much later, after the birth of the only boy she ever had. To her anxious questions concerning the sex of the prematurely born infant she never got any satisfactory reply, and though she might have suspected the truth, yet it was not revealed to her at the time. She was only adjured to take care of herself and to avoid every kind of fatigue, a difficult thing to do, considering the fact that the Russian Sovereigns were about to start for a tour of visits at the different European Courts. These visits, with the exception of the stay in Paris where they were received with a burst of the most extraordinary enthusiasm ever witnessed in the French capital, did not turn out so successfully as had been hoped and expected. For one thing, Prince Lobanoff, who held the portfolio of Foreign Affairs and was by common consent considered as the ablest statesman in Russia and one of the cleverest in Europe, died suddenly on the Imperial train at a little station of the Southwestern Railway line, called Schepétowka, almost in the arms of the Emperor. Nicholas, seeing him stagger, rushed to his help. This sad event gave rise to many comments, and it was then that people began to whisper in Russia that the young Empress had got the evil eye and brought bad luck to all those who came into too close contact with her.

Nicholas and his Consort first proceeded to Breslau, where William II. with the Empress came to meet them and received them with the greatest cordiality. It was at that time that arrangements for his correspondence with the Czarina were made, much to the joy of the latter, who, as time went on, felt more and more in need of the help and advice of members of her own family. From Breslau, the Emperor and Empress proceeded to Vienna, but there a succession of unpleasant small incidents, insignificant in themselves, but destined in the course of time to bring about totally unexpected results, took place. Francis Joseph had decided to receive his Russian guests with all the pomp and splendor for which the Austrian Court had always been famous, and the Empress Elisabeth, after much pleading, had at last been persuaded to come to Vienna and to do the honors of the Hofburg to them. At the State banquet which was given there, she appeared, regal and magnificent, clothed in that deep mourning which she never gave up after the tragic death of her only son, the Archduke Rudolph, and she was far more observed and looked at than the young wife of Nicholas II., who resented the fact deeply. It is not generally known that at that time (later she outlived the feeling) Alexandra Feodorowna had a very high opinion of her own beauty and could not bear to play second fiddle in that respect to any one. She always hated pretty women whenever she saw them in a position to rival her, and the fact that Elisabeth of Bavaria, in spite of her fifty-seven years, eclipsed in many respects her own young and radiant beauty did not help to put the Czarina into a good temper. The interview, therefore, passed according to the rules of strict courtesy, but no cordiality permeated it. Wise politicians and diplomats began shaking their heads and murmuring that after this experiment it would become hard indeed to bring about pleasant relations between the Court of the Hofburg and that of Tsarskoye Selo.

From Vienna, the Russian Sovereigns went on to Copenhagen to pay to the aged King and Queen of Denmark their respects, but there also things did not go smoothly. The Russian Imperial Family had always been popular in Denmark, which the late Czar Alexander III. liked extremely, and where he used to spend happy weeks every summer. One had hoped that this tradition would continue, but after having seen Alexandra Feodorowna for three days Queen Louise had remarked that it would be just as well if she did not visit too often.

But what everybody in Russia looked forward to was the visits which Nicholas II. and his wife were about to pay to Balmoral and to Paris. In the first of these places they were made the objects of a warm and entirely homelike reception on the part of Queen Victoria. The latter had always been interested in the children of her favorite daughter, the Princess Alice, and had immensely rejoiced to see her youngest grandchild ascend the Throne of Russia. The Queen, however, was beginning to feel some misgivings as to the latter's fitness for the high position that she had been thrust into. She was perhaps the best informed person in Europe as to all that went on in Foreign Courts, and she had heard, not without serious apprehensions, of the growing unpopularity of Alexandra Feodorowna. She took the first opportunity which presented itself to talk seriously to her granddaughter and to try and persuade her that she ought to make some effort to win the respect and the affection of her subjects. To Victoria's surprise, the old lady never having been thwarted or contradicted, the Czarina replied that she did not know in the least what she was talking about, and that what Russians required was not amiable words but a sound administration of the whip. Under these circumstances the conversation very quickly came to an end, though the Queen, astounded as she was at Alexandra's impertinence, tried, nevertheless, to renew it with the Czar. The latter simply replied that his grandmother must have been misinformed, because everybody loved the Empress. After that Victoria gave up the subject, and she would probably never have mentioned it to any one had it not subsequently reached her ears that the Empress boasted among her friends about the way in which she had snubbed her grandmother. This was rather more than the equanimity of the Queen could stand, and in her turn she related her unsuccessful attempts to make the young Czarina listen to reason, not making any secret of the fact that the future of the latter filled her with the greatest apprehensions.

In Paris, the Empress found herself more at her ease. Flattery was poured down upon her in buckets. All the newspapers praised her looks, her jewels, her general demeanor, and it was only here and there that a dissenting voice was raised, as in the person of a dressmaker who remarked on the want of taste which had presided at the confection of the dresses with which Alexandra Feodorowna tried to astonish the Parisian natives. On the whole the visit was a success, and it inspired with new zeal all the promoters of the Franco-Russian alliance, among whom the Empress was most certainly not to be reckoned.

Very soon after this triumphal journey, a second child was born to Nicholas II. and his wife; another girl, to the intense disappointment of everybody. I am informed that the first words of Alexandra Feodorowna upon being told of the sex of the infant were:

"What will the nation say, what will it say?"

As a fact the nation said nothing; it had already begun to lose interest in the family affairs of its rulers.

As time went on this indifference to the joys and the woes of the Reigning House grew and grew, until at last it became a recognized fact in the whole of Russia that, as far as Nicholas II. was concerned, whatever happened to him or to his relatives was an object which presented no interest whatever to the millions of Russian men and women, who all of them were looking forward for a change in the destinies and the Government of their country. When he had ascended the Throne, any amount of expectations had been connected with him and with his name. These were very quickly dashed to the ground by his first public speech—the one which he made in reply to the congratulations of the zemstvos, or Russian local assemblies, on his accession and marriage, when he told the representatives of these institutions that they must not indulge "in senseless dreams" or hope that he would ever sacrifice the least little bit of his Imperial prerogatives or autocratic leanings. The Revolutionary committees, which had begun at that time and from the very day of the death of Alexander III. to renew their political activity, addressed to him a letter which, read to-day in the light of the events which have happened during the last twelvemonth, seems almost prophetic. They warned him that the struggle begun by him would only come to an end with his downfall, and the whole tone of this remarkable epistle, which I have reproduced in my volume, *Behind the Veil of the Russian Court*, reminds one at present that the prophesied blow has fallen, of the writing on the wall which appeared during the banquet of the Persian King, warning him of his approaching ruin.

Neither the Czar nor his Consort thought about these things. As time went on, the attention of the latter became more and more concentrated on the one fixed idea of having a son. She imagined that the secret of her unpopularity, which she had at last discovered, lay in the fact that she had not been able to give an Heir to the Russian Throne. Four times in succession daughters were born to her, each one received with increased disappointment, as the years went on, bringing into prominence the youngest brother of Nicholas II., the Grand-Duke Michael, whom the Empress began hating with all her heart and soul. She imagined that wherever she went she was greeted with reproaches for having failed to fulfil the first duty of a Sovereign's Consort, that of assuring his succession in the direct line. The hysterical part of her temperament rose to the surface more and more with each day that passed. She locked herself up in her private apartments, refusing to see the members of her family and denying herself to all visitors, until at last it began to be whispered in Court circles that Alexandra Feodorowna's mind was getting unhinged and that she was suffering from religious mania, mixed up with the dread of persecution from her relatives. She used to sob for hours at a stretch, when no one could comfort her, and during those attacks of despair one cry continually escaped her lips, and was repeated until she could utter it no longer, out of sheer excitement and fatigue:

"Why, *why* will God not grant me a son?"

CHAPTER VI

THE EMPRESS'S OPINIONS ABOUT RUSSIA

ONE of the points about which there has been the most discussion in Russia is as to whether the Empress Alexandra had ever cared for the country which had become her own. Her friends have repeatedly asserted that she had become an ardent Russian patriot, and that her great, particular misfortune was that every action, word, or thought of hers had been misunderstood and this willingly.

As for her enemies, they declared, from the very first days which followed upon her unlucky marriage, that she had arrived in Russia imbued with the feelings of the deepest contempt for the country and its people, and that all her efforts had been applied toward making out of the Empire over which she reigned a vassal of her own native land.

It seems to me, who have had the opportunity to approach her personally, as well as that of hearing about her from persons who nourished no animosity against her, that neither the one nor the other of these two opinions was absolutely correct, though both were right, each in its way. When one attempts to judge the personality and the character of Alexandra Feodorowna, one must first of all take into account the fact that she belonged to that class of individuals who, while being fools, nevertheless think themselves clever. To this must be added a highly strung, hysterical temperament and the fact which was unknown in Russia at the time of her marriage, that madness was a family disease in the House of Hesse, to which she belonged by birth. The circumstances attending her rearing and education also had a good deal to do with the strangeness of her conduct after she had reached the years of discretion. She had been a mere baby, five or six years old, when she had lost her mother, the charming, clever, and accomplished Princess Alice of Great Britain, and she had been brought up partly at Windsor by Queen Victoria and partly at Darmstadt, where, however, she had not found any of the good examples its Court might have afforded her had her mother remained alive. She was the youngest member of her family, and as such treated with negligence and made to give way to her elder sisters, who were neither kind nor affectionate in regard to her—a fact which must have helped her a good deal to develop the haughty, disagreeable temper which was later on to play her so many bad tricks in life. On the other hand, the person who had charge of her education, as well as of that of the other Princesses, had conceived a great and most ill-advised affection for her; ill-advised in so far that she used to repeat to her that she was handsomer and cleverer than her sisters, and that she ought not to mind any slights which the latter might try to put upon her, because she was sure to make a better marriage than they.

When she was about twelve years old there occurred in the Grand-Ducal Palace of Darmstadt the tragedy or romance, call it as one likes, of the Grand Duke's morganatic union with a lovely Russian, Madame Kolémine, which came to such a sad end, owing to the interference of Queen Victoria and to the stupidity of the Grand Duke himself, who, in any case, ought first of all to have made careful inquiries as to the past life and conduct of his intended bride, and then—once he had plighted his troth to her—to have held the promises which he had made to her. He allowed her to be sent away from his Court and country in disgrace; the lady herself would have been but too willing to come to honorable terms with a man for whom she could no longer feel any esteem or affection, because in the whole long story of his intercourse with her Grand-Duke Louis never showed himself otherwise than the true German he really was. Of course, the object of his transient affections was represented to his children as being merely an intriguing, base woman who had tried to make a great marriage and to supplant their mother. Whether the elder Darmstadt Princesses believed this calumny to have been the truth remains a matter of doubt. Judging impartially, this would seem to be hardly likely if one takes into consideration the fact that their ages hovered between eighteen and twenty-two, and that consequently one could reasonably assume that they knew what they were about when they showered one proof of affection after another on Madame Kolémine, and when they declared to her in many letters that there was nothing they wished for more than to see her become their father's wife.

This whole story, together with its heroine, is about one of the most perplexing affairs that ever occurred in any Royal House, and everything connected with it is to this very day shrouded in mystery. Madame Kolémine, who (this by the way) married again, after her divorce from the Grand Duke, a Russian diplomat, may or may not have been a bad woman. I hold no brief for or against her. Many people assert that in regard to certain scandals connected with the time of her early married life she was more sinned against than sinning, and that she became the victim of calumnies launched against her by unscrupulous enemies. But, true or not, the breath of suspicion had hovered around her good name to a sufficiently strong degree to have absolutely justified the objections of Queen Victoria to her becoming even the morganatic wife of the Grand Duke of Hesse.

It ought also to have influenced the latter into not admitting the fascinating Russian into the intimacy of his young daughters, which was precisely what he did. The girls could not be told every kind of gossip going about in the world, but they ought to have been shielded from the possibility of contracting friendships likely to lead them into unpleasantnesses in the future. On the other hand, considering the fact that this intimacy had once been established, one does not very well see how any of the Darmstadt Princesses could have been led to believe, after the three years or more that it had lasted, that Madame Kolémine was base and intriguing and cared only for a great marriage. Because this last accusation, leaving aside all others, was absolutely false, a fact no one was better able to know than themselves, who had repeatedly begged and implored her to accept their father's offer and to make him, together with themselves, happy people.

I have had some of these letters in my hands, and can therefore vouch for the truth of this last assertion, and to put an end to the questions of a suspicious public that may wonder how it came that such a correspondence was ever communicated to me, I will say at once that the reason for it was that I am a blood relation of Madame Kolémine, who after her divorce had thought I might be of some help to her in her troubles, and had herself asked me to read them. The impossibility in which I found myself to be of any use to the poor woman, whom I had never seen in my life before, and of interfering in a business which did not concern me in the very least, led her to take a most bitter attitude in regard to me and to become my enemy, so that in trying to take her part to-day I am doing so out of a feeling of justice and nothing else.

I have mentioned the story in general only because it explains to a certain degree the undisguised aversion of the Empress Alexandra for everything that was Russian or that had anything to do with Russia. She had never shared her sisters' admiration for Madame Kolémine; on the contrary, she had always nourished a pronounced antipathy for the lady, and whatever the three other Darmstadt Princesses may have felt in regard to the woman whom their father was to marry and divorce on the same day, she, at least, had made no secret of her hatred for her. One of the first remarks which she made after she had become acquainted with St. Petersburg society was:

"I shall never like it; all the women remind me of Madame Kolémine."

This episode in the career of the Grand Duke of Hesse brought about, as might have been expected, a change in his relations with Queen Victoria, and he was no longer such a desired guest at Windsor or Balmoral as had been the case. His elder daughters married in quick succession, the second one wedding the Grand-Duke Sergius of Russia. The little Alice was left alone at home, and though she was often requested by her grandmother to join her in England, she did not care so much for these invitations as formerly. The fact was that she was gradually acquiring a considerable influence over her father's mind, whose weakness of intellect rendered him an easy tool in his enterprising daughter's hands. She became the virtual mistress of his house, and developed during those years, where she remained absolutely without any feminine control over her, the imperious, disagreeable temper which was to play her such sorry tricks in the future. Small as was the Hessian Court, it yet was administered with that strict respect for etiquette always in vogue in Germany, and it pleased the Princess Alix to find herself the first lady in the land in her father's Dukedom. She preferred it to being the second in Rome.

It was during those years that she was taken on a visit to the Russian Court. This did not turn out a success, because no one in St. Petersburg was in the very least impressed by the beauty of the young girl. Russia, being celebrated for the loveliness of its women, would have required something more than she possessed to fall on its knees and worship her. Then, again, she was dressed with bad taste, her manners left much to be desired, and the rumor which began to circulate at the time of the possibility of her wedding the Heir to the Russian Throne did not appeal to public feeling. Alice thought herself slighted, and returned to her beloved Darmstadt more anti-Russian than she had ever been.

Two years went by, and the Grand Duke of Hesse died, carried off by a disease of the brain, difficult to account for if one takes into consideration the fact that he had never had any brains to lose. His son succeeded him, and, together with his sister, continued to inhabit the Darmstadt Palace, where nothing was changed except the master of the house, whom no one missed. For eighteen months Princess Alice reigned supreme, as she had done before; then one fine morning her brother announced to her that he was about to ask their cousin, the Princess Victoria Mélita of Coburg, to become his wife. A fit of hysterics followed upon this announcement. Alice could not resign herself to the necessity of playing second fiddle at her brother's Court, where she had been the center of attraction for such a long time. The fact that her future sister-in-law was just as young and more beautiful than she did not help her to get over her mortification. She was of a terribly jealous character and temperament, and she began from that very day to hate, with a ferocious hatred which went on increasing as time passed, the innocent girl for whom this Hessian marriage was to prove the source of so much sorrow. But about this I shall speak later on.

It was at this precise moment that talk about a Russian marriage for her began again. Many people wished for it. The Berlin Court was actively intriguing in favor of it, and during the whole of that winter of 1893-94 the newspapers were busy with it. The chancelleries of the different European capitals were very much preoccupied as to whether or not it would take place.

Perhaps few people will believe me when I say that had it not been for her brother's engagement nothing in the world would have ever decided the Princess Alice to give her consent to a union for which she did not feel the least sympathy. She was not at all dazzled by the prospect of becoming the Empress of Russia, because in her vanity and with her ideas of German grandeur she thought herself far superior to the Romanoffs, thanks to her long and unbroken line of ancestry. Her unimpeachable quarterings seemed to her to be so immeasurably above their doubtful ones that she considered it would be she who would do him an incommensurable honor by accepting as her wedded husband the Heir to the Throne of All the Russias. She would have infinitely preferred going on queening it in Darmstadt, or in any other small German town, than to have been chosen as the bride of the future Nicholas II., for whom she felt neither sympathy, affection, nor esteem.

But her brother's prospective marriage changed considerably her position. She would no longer occupy the position of the first lady of her beloved Hesse; she would find installed in the place which had been her own for so many happy years a woman younger than herself, with an independent character, a determined mind, a woman who would most probably grow very quickly to impose herself and her ways of thinking, not only on the whole Hessian Court, but also on the Grand Duke, whose sister was condemned beforehand to be neglected and treated as a negligible quantity.

This was gall and wormwood to the passionate, selfish girl, and this feeling of hers, which she allowed her cousin the Kaiser to guess, was very cleverly exploited by the latter in view of a marriage which none desired more ardently than himself. Next to his own sister, there was no one in the whole world whom he would have more ardently wished to become Empress of Russia than his cousin Alix. He invited himself to Darmstadt for a short visit, and while there took the first opportunity to discuss the subject with her. He told her what very few people knew at the time, and what the general public was entirely ignorant of—the serious nature of the illness with which Alexander III. was attacked, an illness which gave no hope whatever of recovery. By marrying the young Grand-Duke Nicholas the Princess would find herself but for a short time in a so to say subordinate position. A few months would see her raised to one of the greatest thrones in Europe, from the height of which she would be enabled to look down with contempt and pity on the cousin who was about to take at the Darmstadt Court the place she had occupied so long she had grown to consider it as her very own.

Moreover, she would be able to win back Russia and its ruler to the cause of the German alliance, and thus accomplish one of her duties as a loyal German woman. He appealed to her worst instincts while seeming to call on her noblest ones to assert themselves, and once more he won the day.

In St. Petersburg, too, Hohenzollern influence and intrigues had worked actively, until at last the Czar, feeling perhaps that his days were numbered and perhaps also no longer strong enough to resist perfidious advice given to him by interested people, yielded the point, and when his eldest son started for Coburg to attend there the Princess Victoria Mélita's wedding, he authorized him to ask for the hand of Alix of Hesse.

As I have related, the marriage was at once announced, and we have seen already its first results. The reason why I have once more returned to its subject was to explain some of the causes which led the Empress Alexandra to conceive such a bad opinion about Russia, and to detest so cordially the Russian people. Her early dislike for Madame Kolémine had given her a natural antipathy for everything connected with the latter country; her visits there had strengthened this feeling; her vanity had been hurt by finding that St. Petersburg's society had paid absolutely no attention to her; and her slow, commonplace mind had been utterly unable to understand the refinement and high breeding of the Russian upper classes. Her natural coldness and ignorance had been repulsed instead of attracted by the simplicity but genuine kind-heartedness of the lower ones. She thought the nation one of savages and she made no secret whatever of that opinion, expressing her intention of correcting those "awful Russian manners," which had seemed to her young and inexperienced eyes so very dreadful when she had first become acquainted with them.

It is most likely that if she had married a small German Prince or Potentate she would have put herself out of the way to please his subjects. But she did not think the Russians worth her while. She considered that they ought to feel themselves highly honored by the fact that she had consented to come and reign over them, and in her own mind she did not attach any more importance to the judgments they might be inclined to bestow in regard to her person than she would have done to the criticisms of the first beggar in the street. She arrived in her new country despising it, together with its people, determined to ignore the wishes it might have or the necessities it might require. She arrived there prejudiced and bigoted, and so full of contempt for the land that hailed her as its Queen that she did not admit the possibility of treating it as one inhabited by human beings, but determined to apply to it some of the methods used by the Germans in their treatment of their Colonies.

For the opinion held by Alix of Hesse-Darmstadt in regard to Russia was simply that it ought to be nothing else but a Colony of the vast German Empire, and she felt more pride at the thought that she might reduce it to this condition than at the idea that she had been chosen out of so many other women to become the Empress of that Realm.

CHAPTER VII

WHAT THE IMPERIAL FAMILY THOUGHT ABOUT THE EMPRESS

IT would not have been human on the part of the Imperial Family to like the young wife of Nicholas II. in those early days which followed upon her marriage. The feminine portion of it especially could have been expected, before even the wedding of Alexandra Feodorowna had been solemnized, to look upon her with eyes full of criticism and with the desire to find fault with whatever she might say or do. Here she was, a young, lovely girl, in the full bloom of her beauty, put into the place of the first lady in the Realm, at a moment's notice, before even she had gone through that period of probation which falls as a general rule to the lot of every Consort of a Sovereign when she is but the wife of the Heir to the Throne. Had the haughty Imperial ladies, who for so many years had ruled according to their fancies St. Petersburg society, found themselves in presence of a Grand-Duchess Czarevna whom they would have been able to advise, scold, or pet, according to their fancy, they might have taken, from the height of their own unassailable positions, a more indulgent view of her unavoidable mistakes. They would have thought of her as of a young niece who owed them respect and submission, and whom it was their duty to train according to the exigencies of Russian etiquette. It must be remembered that Nicholas II. to the very day of his accession had been treated by his family like a mere boy without any importance. All of a sudden he found himself a Sovereign and, what was even worse, his wife, the little Hessian Princess, upon whom everybody had looked down with pity mixed with contempt, was the Empress of All the Russias. This was more than the Romanoffs could endure, especially when they remembered the cool, authoritative manner which the late Czar Alexander III. had always adopted in regard to them, and when they thought it might be possible his successor would imitate him in that respect at least, if not in others.

They need not have been in any apprehension as to this last point. Nicholas II., though he detested his uncles, yet stood in such awe of them that he would never have dared assert himself in their presence, far less contradict them. But the Empress had a different character, and she very quickly realized that all her relatives were furious at the fact of her being placed so far above them in rank and position. Fully conscious as she was of that rank, she determined that she would use its advantages to crush those in whom she saw but enemies, which in some cases was not quite exact, because there were then still some persons who, had she only appealed to them, would have responded to her call for sympathy and put themselves at her disposal, if only out of the motive that in rallying around her they were at the same time establishing their own influence.

Alexandra had no tact, and she never could hide her feelings in regard to the people who surrounded her. This explains the number of her enemies and the antagonism to which her mere presence anywhere gave rise. She knew very well that it would be very hard, if not impossible, for her to overcome certain prejudices existing against her. Instead, however, of trying to make for herself friends in other circles than purely aristocratic ones, she applied herself to wound those in whom she saw adversaries, and to discourage her friends by her utter disregard of the warnings that the latter sometimes thought it their duty to give to her. Her relations with the Empress Dowager had begun by being very cordial and affectionate, and it was she who had proposed to the Czar to take their abode in the Anitchkoff Palace with his mother, until their own apartments in the Winter Palace had been got ready for them. The arrangement had not been a successful one, and it is probable that Marie Feodorowna would have got on better later on with her daughter-in-law had the two ladies not lived under the same roof for about half a year. As it was they grew to know each other "not wisely, but too well," and the result was profound contempt on one side and sullen anger on the other. Servants' gossip did the rest; and the two incidents which I have already described, concerning the Crown Jewels and the liturgy, added the last drop of venom in a cup already full to overflowing. The Dowager began to criticize discreetly the young Empress, together with some of her intimate friends. These did not scruple to repeat what they had heard to their own near chums, and soon it became common property. The Grand Duchesses took their cue from Marie Feodorowna, and in an underhand way lamented over the failings of "dear Alexandra," her coldness, her want of politeness, and so forth, helping her in the mean while as much as they could to accentuate the shortcomings of an attitude which very soon came to displease everybody, even the people who had been the most enthusiastic about the young Empress.

As a proof of this fact I will relate a little incident which, at the time it occurred, proved the subject of much gossip in some select circles of St. Petersburg society. During one of the first receptions held at the Winter Palace, after the marriage of Nicholas II., there made her appearance an old lady who for the sake of convenience we shall call Madame A. She wished to be presented to the new Empress, an honor to which her own position, together with that of her late husband, gave her every right, besides the fact that she was one of the few ladies left in the capital who had adhered to the old Russian custom of keeping open house for her friends, and whose *salon* was a social authority in its way. The Empress, upon being shown the list of the people about to be presented to her, wanted to know who they were, and, seeing near her her aunt, the Grand-Duchess Marie Pawlowna, the wife of the Grand-Duke Wladimir, asked her whether Madame A. was or was not a person of importance. The Grand Duchess, who for reasons of her own disliked the latter, replied to her niece:

"Oh, she is an old frump. Give her your hand to kiss, and she will be satisfied."

Now this was the one thing which would not have satisfied Madame A. at all, who considered herself entitled to quite special consideration. Alexandra Feodorowna, believing her aunt, executed the latter's advice to the letter. She extended her much-bejeweled fingers to the astonished old lady, and then coolly turned her back upon her and passed on without having said one single word. The scandal was immense, so immense that the whole ballroom rang with it within a few minutes, and one of the Empress's ladies in waiting actually went up to her and tried to enlighten her as to the extent of the enormity which she had committed, advising her at the same time to seek out the irate Madame A. and to make her some kind of apology, under the pretext that she had not heard her name when it had been mentioned to her.

Alexandra Feodorowna in her turn, and with a certain amount of reason, became furious against the Grand-Duchess Marie Pawlowna for having thus led her into a snare, and, boiling with rage, she crossed the room, went up to where Madame A. was discussing with volubility, together with some of her friends, the slight to which she had been subjected, and told her quite loudly:

"I am sorry, Madame, not to have treated you with the respect to which you are entitled, but it was the Grand-Duchess Marie Pawlowna, my aunt, who had advised me to do it."

One may imagine the effect produced by this short sentence, which, instead of soothing the ruffled feelings of Madame A., added to her indignation. She turned round and replied quite distinctly, so that all the people standing near her heard her plainly:

"Ce n'est pas à l'aide d'une trahison, Madame, que l'on excuse une impolitesse!" ("It is not with the help of a treachery, Madame, that one can excuse a rudeness").

And making a deep courtesy to the discomfited Sovereign, Madame A. proudly retired and drove away from the Palace, leaving the Empress with the consciousness that in the space of five short minutes she had contrived to make for herself two mortal enemies.

The whole of the Imperial Family took up the cause of the Grand-Duchess Marie Pawlowna. The latter's husband, the Grand-Duke Wladimir, went to the Emperor and complained bitterly of the conduct of Alexandra Feodorowna. The other Grand Duchesses declared that, dating from that day, they would have nothing to do with her, except when the necessities of etiquette compelled them to appear at Court, but that personal relations with a person capable of such a grave piece of indiscretion were quite out of the question. The Grand-Duchess Marie swore that she had never meant to advise her niece to show herself rude to such a respectable personage as Madame A.; that her words had been a mere joke, to which she had never imagined that any importance could be attached, and that it had been a cruel thing to denounce her in such a ruthless way to the worst gossip and most malicious tongue in St. Petersburg.

Even the Dowager Empress expressed herself as shocked beyond words at her daughter-in-law's behavior, but when she had tried to speak with the latter on the subject Alexandra Feodorowna had exclaimed that she recognized the right of no one to criticize her actions, and forthwith produced for her mother-in-law's edification a caricature which she had drawn of the Emperor in swaddling-clothes, seated at a dinner-table in a high-backed chair, with his uncles and aunts standing around him, and threatening him with their fingers, adding that she was not going to follow the example of her spouse, and that if he chose to forget before his relatives that he was the Emperor of All the Russias, she would not do so for one single minute. After this the conversation came to an end, as was to be expected, but its consequences survived, with a vengeance into the bargain.

Of course incidents of the kind could not be productive of good relations. It did not take a long while before the general public, which, at that time, looked very much for its inspirations toward the Imperial Family, had come to the conclusion that the young Empress was a capricious, rude, and most disagreeable kind of person to whom it was preferable to give a wide berth. Once this legend had been transferred into the domain of history, every action, every word, every gesture of Alexandra Feodorowna was watched with attentive and critical eyes, always ready to make capital out of all her mistakes and to amplify all her errors into crimes. The fact of her having no son added to the resentful feelings of the nation against her, and that of her undisguised German sympathies did not contribute to make her popular. She in her turn, angry with her family, furious with St. Petersburg society, unable to seek friends among the Russian people, all of whom seemed in her inexperienced and prejudiced eyes to be more or less savage, set herself a task to show her contempt and dislike to those persons whom she had found so ready to throw stones against her on occasions when her conscience had told her that she did not deserve the insult. She retired more and more into the seclusion and privacy of her home at Tsarskoye Selo, and she announced to whoever wished to hear her that she did not see why she should spend her money in giving balls and entertaining a society that seemed to have made up its mind to insult her on every possible occasion. The words were repeated, and immediately taken up by the public in the light of another affront. One declared that for a penniless Hessian Princess to talk about "her money" was, to say the least, ridiculous, and one added that she ought to remember that it was part of the duties of a Russian Empress to entertain her subjects and to give them some pleasures in return for their fidelity.

Such was the position after Alexandra Feodorowna had been married three or four years. She might still at that time, had she attempted it in earnest, won back at least the respect if not the sympathies of the Russian nation. But to do so she would have had to bend down from the height of the Throne upon which she was seated, and to make some efforts to clear the misunderstandings which had arisen between her, her family, and her subjects. Unfortunately for her, the haughty Princess believed so firmly that she had been sinned against without having the least sin to her own credit that this "injustice," as she called it, in the world's judgments of her personality made her rebellious, and, not being clever enough either to forgive or to disdain it, she could find nothing else to do but to seek to revenge herself upon imaginary wrongs by making herself guilty of real ones.

CHAPTER VIII

SORROW AND UNEXPECTED CONSOLATION

IT was not only her family and St. Petersburg society with whom the Empress could not agree. Her relations with her husband were also not of the best during the first years of her married life. Later on, when Alexandra Feodorowna had fallen into the hands of the clever gang of adventurers whose tool she was to remain until the final catastrophe which drove her from her Throne had taken place, she contrived to get hold of the feeble mind of Nicholas II., and to influence him absolutely, thanks to his love for his children, especially for his son.

During the first five years or so that followed upon his marriage the Czar, though he never quarreled with his wife, yet thought far less about her than he did about his mistress, the dancer Mathilde Krzesinska, a Pole of extreme intelligence, little beauty, but enormous attraction. Their friendship had begun when Nicholas was but a boy, or about that, rumor would have it, though I have reason for knowing that in this rumor was mistaken, as happens so often to the old lady, that the dancer had been chosen by the Empress Marie herself as a fit friend for her eldest son. The fact was that this liaison had started almost immediately after the Grand Duke's return from his journey round the world, which had had such a dramatic incident to enliven it in Japan, when a fanatic had attempted to take the life of the Heir to the Russian Throne, inflicting upon him a deep wound with his sword.

The Cesarewitsch had seen Mademoiselle Krzesinska on the stage of the Marinsky Theater, and had been very much impressed by her talent and grace. He had asked to be introduced to her, and had forthwith carried her off to supper at a fashionable restaurant called Cubat, where all the *jeunesse dorée* of St. Petersburg used to meet, eat, drink, and be merry. This supper, in which had taken part several of Nicholas's friends, officers in the same Hussar regiment where he was a captain, as well as one or two ladies of great beauty and doubtful reputation, had ended in a scandal, which for several weeks had been almost the only subject of discussion in the aristocratic *salons* of the capital. The company had been enjoying itself so much that glasses and plates had been broken; when, at two o'clock in the morning, the owner of the restaurant had ventured to suggest that it would be high time the entertainment came to an end, he had been sent to mind his own business. This the poor man would have been but too glad to do, but police regulations were very strict at that time, and he knew that if a patrol should see light in his windows from the outside that he would be fined heavily, no matter who had elected to remain in his establishment after the curfew had sounded.

The Czar

This was precisely what happened.

A police officer walked up and knocked at the door of the private room where the Heir to the Russian Throne and his companions were disporting themselves, and ordered them to get out. The Grand Duke's aide-de-camp did not care to disclose the identity of his master, so he came out alone and tried to remonstrate with the man, asking him to give them another half-hour to finish their supper and pay for it. The officer refused and tried to force his way into the room, but was violently thrust aside. He had not the right to enforce his authority against a colonel in the army, which was the rank of the aide-de-camp, so he withdrew and telephoned to the Prefect of the town, General Wahl. The latter, who was an officious busybody, thought it a splendid occasion to assert his authority. He immediately proceeded himself to Cubat, where, in spite of the efforts made by the companions of the Grand Duke to keep him out, he rushed into the room, to find himself confronted by the Heir to the Throne. Nicholas became very angry and asked the General how he dared intrude upon his privacy. Wahl, furious in his turn, retorted that it was his duty to see that order was maintained in the capital, no matter who was troubling it, upon which, in one of the uncontrollable fits of rage to which he was sometimes subject, the Cesarewitsch seized hold of a dish full of caviar which stood on the table and threw its contents in the face of Wahl. A scene of indescribable disorder followed. At last Prince Bariatinsky, one of the generals in waiting on the Czar, who had accompanied the young Grand Duke during the latter's journey round the world, was sent for. He succeeded in putting an end to an incident which reflected credit upon none of those who had taken part in it.

The next day Alexander III. was apprised of what had taken place. History does not say what he told his son, but it was supposed that it had not been anything in the way of praise, because there was nothing that the Emperor hated more than a drunken brawl, and it must have been very painful for him to find that his Heir had become involved in one. But when General Wahl arrived, full of complaints and indignation at the treatment to which he had been subjected, the Monarch expressed to him his entire disapproval of his conduct, saying that he had had no right to intrude upon the privacy of the Grand Duke, and that he ought not to have forgotten the immense difference of rank which existed between him and the future Emperor of Russia. Wahl did not require to be told twice the same thing, and in the future he never attempted to interfere with the pleasures of any member of the Imperial Family.

People who were present at this ill-fated supper told afterward, when relating all the incidents which had made it a memorable one, that Nicholas wished to do something worse than pour the contents of a caviar-dish on General Wahl's head, but that Mademoiselle Krzesinska had thrown herself between them. True or not, it is certain that after this night the Grand Duke took to visiting the beautiful dancer in her home, and very soon their relations became an established fact. She bore him two sons, which gave her distinct advantages over all the other flirtations in which her Imperial lover indulged from time to time, flirtations which she was far too clever and careful to notice. What she aspired to afterward was to become a power in the land, a *Maîtresse de Roi,* such as had been seen at the French Court during the reigns of the last Bourbons. Her Polish propensity for intrigue coming to her help, she very soon contrived to make for herself an excellent position in the world as well as to earn a considerable fortune. She was a very reasonable, matter-of-fact woman; she knew very well that Nicholas had to marry, whether he liked it or not, and her only preoccupation, if we are to believe all that was related in St. Petersburg at the time, was whether he should marry a clever or a stupid woman. It is not difficult to guess the one she would have preferred had the choice been left to her discretion.

When the betrothal of the Cesarewitsch with the Princess Alix of Hesse was announced Mademoiselle Krzesinska, far from objecting to it, applied herself, on the contrary, to persuading him that he had done quite right and that he could not have chosen a better wife. She imagined that the placid German temperament of the bride-to-be would look with innocent eyes on the continuation of her intrigue with Nicholas, in which supposition she was vastly mistaken, because Alice, though she did not care for the husband she had been compelled to marry, did not mean to let him wander away from the conjugal home in search of a happiness she believed herself quite capable of alone procuring for him. She tried to separate the Grand Duke from the clever dancer who held him in her bondage, and of course she failed.

Nicholas kept up his former habits of going to see Mademoiselle Krzesinska whenever he had the time to do so; what was even worse, he continued to consult her on many matters which he never discussed with his wife. The latter became very unhappy, and it was then that even her affection for her children was not sufficient to prevent her from uttering aloud her despair at having been obliged to leave her dear Darmstadt for a country where everything and everybody conspired against her and her peace of mind, and where she could not even win the love of the husband who had been imposed upon her.

Among the few people whom she used to see more frequently than others was the Montenegrin Princess Stana, who had been married to Duke George of Leuchtenberg, with whom she had led a most unhappy, uncanny sort of existence. Stana, like all the Montenegrin daughters of King Nicholas, was a charming and attractive woman, clever into the bargain. In spite of her unhappy conjugal experiences she had grown very fond of Russia, and especially of her position as a member of the Russian Imperial Family. She was very willing to divorce the miserable husband to whom she had been united, who had insulted and outraged her without the least compunction from the very first day of their marriage; but she would have liked to find another one whose affection, and especially whose worldly situation, were such that her future would be assured on even more brilliant lines than the present. Her elder sister, Princess Militza, was the wife of the Grand-Duke Peter Nicholaievitch, whose brother was that Grand-Duke Nicholas who was later on to acquire such a reputation as Commander-in-chief of the Russian armies during the first months of the present war. Grand-Duke Nicholas was not considered as a marriageable man, being bound by ties of close friendship since a good number of years with an attractive woman, Madame Bourénine. Nevertheless, Princess Stana made up her mind to marry him, an enterprise which seemed the more hopeless that it was against the canons of the Greek Orthodox Church for two sisters to marry two brothers. As we have seen, her sister was Grand-Duke Nicholas's sister-in-law.

This, however, did not much trouble the determined Stana, but she knew very well that it would be quite impossible for her to succeed in her designs unless she managed to enlist on her side the sympathies of somebody strong enough to protect her and to lend her the support which she needed. It was useless to think of the Empress Dowager, because the latter had never looked kindly upon the Montenegrin Princesses, to whom she had been very good at the time that they were being brought up in the Smolny Convent in St. Petersburg, and who had rewarded her with the basest ingratitude later on. The Emperor was a mere puppet in the hands of his advisers, and these, Stana knew but too well, would be against any idea of her becoming the wife of Nicholas Nicholaievitch. Remained the young Empress, to whom no one to that day had ever dared to apply for anything, who had been considered by general consent as not being worthy of any attention or consideration. Stana imagined that any proofs of respect which she might give to her were bound to be more appreciated than they would have been under different circumstances. She forthwith proceeded to lay siege with great care and tact to the heart and the sympathies of Alexandra Feodorowna.

At first her advances were met with rebuff; then gradually, seeing how attentive and full of deference her cousin showed herself in respect to her person, the young Empress began to thaw; and soon a friendship, the more surprising that the two ladies did not seem to have anything whatever in common in their respective characters—even a close friendship—established itself between them, and the miserable wife of Nicholas II. poured out the sorrows which racked her heart to the willing ears of Stana Leuchtenberg, who, in her turn, related all her own misfortunes. At last Alexandra interested herself so much in the welfare of this other victim of an unhappy marriage that she exerted all her influence to persuade the Emperor to grant her the permission to sue for a divorce. At the same time she applied herself to invite the Grand-Duke Nicholas as often as possible either at Tsarskoye Selo or at Livadia, and to make him meet there the beautiful Stana Leuchtenberg. The expected happened, and soon poor Madame Bourénine was forgotten, and the betrothal of the Empress's two protégés was announced, much to the indignation of the man in the street, who did not approve of it by any means.

The Grand-Duke Nicholas was in his way just as ambitious a man as the fair Montenegrin he had married. To the Crimea they both repaired as soon as the divorce of the Princess had been pronounced. He knew very well the weakness which characterized his nephew, the Czar, and he would have dearly liked to become the latter's chief adviser and even his Prime Minister. He therefore favored his new wife's intimacy with the Empress, so that the couple were often seen at Tsarskoye Selo, much more so, in fact, than any other members of the Imperial Family.

Now the Grand Duke had one weakness. He believed in spiritualism, in turning tables, and all kinds of superstitious extravagances. The Empress's leanings had also since some time been directed toward the same subject, but she had felt afraid to speak about it, knowing very well that this would not be looked upon with lenient eyes by the Czar or by his mother. When she discovered, however, that Nicholas Nicholaievitch did not feel in the least ashamed if he were caught trying to communicate, through the medium of a table or of a pencil, with the inhabitants of the other world, she confided to him her great desire to do the same thing. The Grand Duke replied that nothing could be easier. They held several séances to which the Emperor also came, attracted by the descriptions which his cousin had made to him. Nicholas Nicholaievitch promised the Empress that he would bring to her a famous French medium called Philippe, who would most certainly make her witness most extraordinary performances in regard to the evocation of the spirits of people dead long before.

Alexandra Feodorowna was delighted. She had already derived great comfort from her intercourse with her cousins, and her feeling of affection for Stana had acquired considerable warmth since the beginning of their friendship. Moreover, she knew that the Grand-Duke Nicholas was considered the strong man in the Romanoff family, and she realized that to have him on her side would be a distinct advantage for her, and that his support might help her to overcome many difficulties. Therefore she appreciated very much all the acts of attention which both Stana and her husband were fond of pouring upon her. When Nicholas told her that he would gratify her wish to see a real medium she was more than delighted. She did not foresee whither this fatal introduction was to lead her, nor realize the ill turn that her cousin was doing her by giving her an opportunity of indulging her tastes for the supernatural, to which she was to owe so many of the misfortunes which were to assail her in later years, and which were to play such an important part in the tragedy that ended with her downfall. She was looking for the consolation of the moment without thinking of the possibility of the catastrophe of the morrow.

CHAPTER IX

PHILIPPE AND HIS WORK

THE Grand-Duke Nicholas kept his word, and one afternoon he brought to Tsarskoye Selo the famous Philippe, about whom his wife had spoken so often and with such enthusiasm to the young Empress. Before relating what followed upon this hasty and ill-advised introduction of an adventurer in the family circle of the Czar, it may not be out of place to say a few words concerning this personage, as well as to give a short description of his person.

Philippe was a Frenchman who, if all that has been related about him is true, had come to grief in his native land, to which he had thought it wiser to bid good-by for a time at least. He had spent several years in Germany, studying at German universities (at least he said so) and had given a great deal of attention to occultism and everything connected with it. Why he came to St. Petersburg no one ever knew, and though he has been accused of having tried from the very first months of his arrival in Russia to get introduced to the Sovereigns, yet I do not personally believe in this part of the story, because at that time no one suspected Alexandra Feodorowna or Nicholas II. of being interested in the supernatural. What is more likely is that he only attempted to get acquainted with the aristocratic circles of the capital, some of which were known to be attracted by these manifestations which begin by turning tables and end in more or less genuine hysteria. Later on when it became known that the Emperor and Empress themselves had given a welcome to the spiritualistic doctrines which Philippe preached, it is probable that the idea was suggested to him, by people who realized what capital might be made out of this circumstance, that he might come to acquire political influence, if he would but make use of his science to enslave the weak persons who had come to believe in him.

Personal ambition and vanity did the rest, combined with a good deal of German money, cleverly and judiciously spent in the furtherance of deep schemes, the real purport of which he was never allowed to suspect. He was encouraged to consider himself as a personage of great importance, and one upon whose shoulders rested some of the responsibilities which, properly speaking, belonged to the Czar alone. He was clever, bright, and assimilated very quickly all that he heard or saw, and knew how to turn to the best advantage every possible circumstance with which his personal welfare or interest was connected. As soon as he found himself in the presence of Alexandra Feodorowna he understood how easy it would be for him to get hold of a mind which he judged at once, and this quite rightly, not to be well balanced. He therefore played upon it; he ministered to it; he took advantage of it and of its vagaries; and he soon acquired over the young Sovereign an influence such as no one before him had ever wielded, and such as no one in the future was to have, with the exception of the famous Raspoutine of evil memory.

At first Philippe proceeded with great caution—so great, indeed, as to elude even the suspicious eyes of the Grand-Duke Nicholas, who, though he had been instrumental in bringing this impostor to Court, yet would not at all have liked to see him become influential there, and who watched him very carefully during the séances which were held every Saturday evening at Tsarskoye Selo. Even the suspicious eyes of the Grand-Duke Nicholas could not detect anything the least dangerous in his manner of proceeding. Philippe acted the medium to perfection. He used to go into regular trances, during which he replied to the various questions put to him with more or less accuracy; he never could be detected, once he was awake again, as having the slightest knowledge or remembrance of what had taken place while he had been asleep. Several times he prophesied with such exactitude that it seemed marvelous.

On one of these occasions he announced to the small circle assembled to listen to him in the Empress's boudoir that a serious misfortune was threatening the State through the death of one of its most important functionaries. He was still plunged in the hypnotic sleep during which he made this startling announcement when Count Lamsdorff, who occupied the position of Under Secretary of State for Foreign Affairs, arrived at Tsarskoye Selo and asked to be received by the Emperor on urgent and important business. He had come to communicate to the Monarch the news of the sudden death that same evening of the Minister for Foreign Affairs, Count Mourawieff. Of course this set the seal to Philippe's reputation as a prophet. Afterward some meddlesome people assumed that he had become aware of the sad event before he had left St. Petersburg to proceed to the Imperial country Palace by one of those singular accidents which happen sometimes in life, and that he had very intelligently made use of this knowledge during the trance in which he had pretended to be plunged. True or not, the story circulated freely, and was repeated everywhere, but the people who ought to have been the most interested in it did not, of course, hear it. On the contrary, the influence of the impostor was considerably strengthened by the incident, even in regard to the Grand-Duke Nicholas, who from that moment began himself to consult Philippe in various matters. Then the Grand Duke had to leave for the Crimea, where he usually spent part of the year, on account of the health of the Grand Duchess, which had never been of the strongest, and he left Philippe in possession of the field.

In spite of Nicholas Nicholaievitch's absence, the séances with the medium continued, and they became even longer and more frequent than had been the case before. The Empress developed more and more interest in their progress, and at last one day, when Philippe asked her whether she would not try to be sent to sleep by him in order to get rid of the cruel headaches from which she suffered, she did not object; on the contrary, expressed herself as quite willing to make the experiment. Philippe, however, insisted on one condition, which was that he should be left alone with her while it proceeded.

Here comes the surprising part of this singular business. Instead of protesting against this pretension of the adventurer, Alexandra Feodorowna accepted it as a matter of course, and, what is more surprising even, she induced the Czar to give his consent. Philippe sent her to sleep, with the result that her headaches really improved and that she began to get into the habit of talking with him, either willingly or unwillingly, about all the events of her daily life and of consulting him whenever she thought that she found herself confronted by any difficulty.

She confided to him—what he knew already—her passionate desire to become the mother of a son, as well as the many disillusions of her married life. Philippe encouraged her, and he was the first one who suggested to her the advisability of taking an interest in public affairs, instead of holding herself aloof from them, and to point out to her the necessity which existed for her, in order to consolidate her personal position, to try and acquire some influence over her husband's mind, and in this way to eliminate that of the Empress Dowager. When Alexandra Feodorowna protested, the adventurer declared to her that he had been sent from heaven to come to her help, that it had been suggested to him by the invisible spirits which always inspired him to go to Russia and to give her the benefit of his experience so as to deliver her from her numerous enemies.

When she declared that she understood nothing about politics, he replied that it was her duty to learn, and that if she did not find any one in Russia willing to teach her, there was her own family in Germany who would be but too glad to come to her rescue, together with their knowledge of the art of government and of handling men and facts. He added that this was the more indispensable that she was about to give birth at last to the son she had been longing for since so many years, and that this son would grow to be an honor to her, as well as the greatest Sovereign Russia had ever known.

Poor infatuated Alexandra believed the adventurer, believed in him so thoroughly that she imagined that she was really about to become a mother once more, and solemnly announced the fact to the Emperor and to the Imperial Family.

Great preparations were made for the auspicious event, and once more the hopes that Nicholas II. might have at last an Heir to his Throne and Crown were awakened. It is related that everything had been got ready, that even the guns which were to announce the birth of a new member of the Romanoff dynasty had been placed on the ramparts of the fortress of SS. Peter and Paul to be fired as soon as the event had taken place, when the suspicions of the Empress Dowager were awakened by the attitude of her daughter-in-law as well as by her physical appearance. She began to watch her, and to do so with the more care. The time for the latter's presumed confinement had passed without that confinement having occurred. Alexandra Feodorowna was observed to be in tears, and her nervous condition became almost alarming, but she refused to see a doctor, and declared that she felt sure she would be better as soon as the suspense under which she was laboring was over. She remained long hours closeted alone with Philippe, who seemed to be the only man capable of bringing some calm to her over-excited system.

Some member of the Court took upon himself the task of writing to the Grand-

Duke Nicholas Nicholaievitch in the Crimea, advising him that something had gone wrong with the Empress, and that Philippe was concerned in it. One must give the Grand Duke his due. He had never meant any harm to his cousin's wife when he had brought the impostor to Court. As we have seen, the latter had been most careful in his whole demeanor while the Grand Duke had remained at hand to control his conduct and his actions. This did not prevent him from rushing back to St. Petersburg as soon as he heard of the strange doings which were shaking the equanimity of the inhabitants of Tsarskoye Selo. He had no sooner seen the Emperor and the Empress than he guessed what had really occurred. He forthwith proceeded to tell the Monarch that the medical attendants of Alexandra Feodorowna must see and examine her, whether she liked it or not, because her state of health was a question which did not interest her alone, but was of the utmost importance to the whole country as well as to the dynasty. He hinted at certain gossip which was going about, to the effect that it was the intention of the Empress to palm off a supposed son on her husband and on his family. Altogether he spoke so strongly that Nicholas II. became seriously alarmed, and for once in his life asserted his authority and compelled his wife to submit to a medical examination.

The result stupefied him as well as other people, because it was ascertained that the hopes of motherhood of Alexandra Feodorowna had only existed in her imagination; that there was no prospect whatever of her giving to Russia that Heir for whose advent the whole country was so eager. Of course the scandal was great, though an attempt was made to soften it by the publication of an official bulletin stating that an unfortunate accident had destroyed the hopes of the Imperial Family. For those who had perforce to become aware of the true circumstances of this whole adventure, the Empress remained under the shadow of a ridicule which was to cling to her for a long time and was not forgotten even when the present war broke out.

The Grand-Duke Nicholas had a stormy interview with Philippe. The impostor pretended that he was not to blame, that the Empress had misunderstood him altogether, and that he, together with the rest of the world, had honestly believed in her supposed hopes of maternity. But in the mean while it had been discovered that during the séances which he had held at Tsarskoye Selo he had mesmerized Alexandra Feodorowna, and abused the confidence she had reposed in him by trying to worm out of her State secrets she was believed to know. The Grand Duke kicked the man out of the Palace, and told him that if he ever dared to set his foot in it again he would have him sent to Siberia under escort. He proceeded to acquaint the Emperor with all that he had discovered and to request the latter to issue orders for the expulsion from Russia of the impostor who had thrown so much ridicule on him as well as on the whole dynasty, who had acquired, thanks to his underhand maneuvers, such a disastrous influence over the mind of his Imperial Consort.

Philippe disappeared and was never seen any more. No one knew what happened to him, or where he was sent, and no one troubled. He had been a nine days' wonder and he sank into oblivion, but the Empress's mad infatuation for him was not forgotten so easily. The more so because she did not attempt to hide her grief at his removal, and bitterly reproached the Grand-Duke Nicholas for his interference in a matter which, as she declared, did not concern him. Angry words were exchanged and the old intimacy which had existed between the Grand-Duchess Stana, her husband, and Alexandra Feodorowna not only came to an end, but was replaced by a hatred the more bitter that it had perforce to be concealed under the veil of politeness and amiability. The Empress's nature, as we know already, was essentially a vindictive one, and the insult, as she considered it, to which she had been subjected on the part of Nicholas Nicholaievitch was to be avenged by her many years later on the day when, thanks to her and to her new favorite, Raspoutine, he was deprived of his position as Commander-in-chief of the Russian armies in the field.

CHAPTER X

ANNA WYRUBEWA APPEARS ON THE SCENE AND HE SAW HER PASS

AFTER the disastrous Philippe incident, the character of the Empress Alexandra changed considerably. She became a sullen, morose, melancholy woman, with a grudge against the world in general and the people with whom she lived in particular. Her sisters-in-law, the Grand-Duchess Xenia Alexandrowna and the Grand-Duchess Olga of Oldenburg, tried to come to her help and to enliven her by attempting to bring her out of the solitude in which she shut herself up, and if she would only have responded to these efforts it is possible that the whole course of her life might have run differently. But the Empress persisted in seeing enemies in everyone of her relatives, and, instead of trying to break through this wall of hostility with which she believed herself surrounded, she used all her powers of persuasion to induce her husband to take the same attitude of antagonism in regard to his family which she had adopted herself. Of course this was not forgiven her.

Nicholas II.'s sisters, who loved him dearly, were affronted when they discovered that their former intimate relations with their brother had come to an end, and that for some reason or other he looked upon them with suspicious eyes. Xenia simply shrugged her shoulders, and, being very wisely advised by her husband, the Grand-Duke Alexander Michaylovitch, who, like all the members of that branch of the Romanoff family, was exceedingly intelligent, refrained from saying anything. But Olga, who was of a more enterprising turn of mind, accosted the Czar one day and talked to him quite seriously about the conduct of the Empress, pointing out to him the harm which she was doing him by her rudeness toward the members of the Imperial Family, and expressing the conviction that times were sufficiently serious. This was during the Japanese war. The Emperor listened to her, as he listened to everybody who spoke to him, with courtesy and attention, but the only reply which she could obtain from him was to the effect that the Empress was in a bad state of health, that her nerves were quite unstrung, and that it would be wrong to take anything she said or did too seriously.

"But you are not nervous or ill," exclaimed the Grand Duchess. "How does it come, then, that you avoid us, your sisters, and even our mother just as much as does your wife. What have we done to you, except to love you, for you to treat us as if we were strangers?"

Nicholas II. pulled his mustache, but would not explain himself further, and Olga Alexandrowna had to own herself baffled.

The Empress heard of this conversation and it did not reconcile her to her sisters-in-law. She was in that morbid state of mind which gives an undue importance to the smallest incident which would not arrest for five minutes the attention of any normal person. The predisposition to insanity which existed in the Hesse-Darmstadt family had probably something to do with her condition, because she most certainly suffered from the mania of persecution; being a Sovereign, and a powerful one into the bargain, she imagined that the best use she could make of her unlimited power was to crush those in whom she persisted in seeing enemies bent on her destruction.

Rumors had reached her ears that some members of the Imperial Family (it had been the Grand-Duke Nicholas Nicholaievitch, in fact) had said that her place ought to be in a convent rather than on the Throne, and she had immediately made out of the remark a desire on the part of her kinsman to shut her up in a monastery, as had been done in the Middle Ages with other Russian Czarinas, so as to give the Emperor the possibility to marry another woman who could bear him a son.

The supposition was a preposterous one, because such an idea had never crossed the Grand Duke's mind, but it could not be driven away out of the imagination of Alexandra Feodorowna. Hence her continual efforts to estrange her husband from his people, and to keep him entirely in her own hands, far away from any influence hostile to herself or to her daughters. There was, after all, some method in her madness. As things turned out, she was given several opportunities to exert her vengeful feelings in regard to the Imperial Family by the conduct of a few of its members.

I will here mention briefly two or three occasions when her intervention caused any amount of trouble and brought upon her head storms of abuse and indignation. The first one was the morganatic marriage of the Grand-Duke Paul, the Emperor's uncle. This event was brought about principally through the want of tact and the stupidity of the people concerned in it, and it would have been far better for the Empress not to have interested herself in it at all, considering the fact that the personages concerned in this affair were certainly beneath her notice.

The Grand Duke had been upon terms of intimate friendship with a lady very well known in social circles of St. Petersburg, the wife of one of the officers of the regiment of which he was the commander. The thing had been going on for a number of years, and society had turned away its head and affected not to notice it; the more so that the husband of the lady in question seemed to ignore it, and to keep his eyes firmly closed as to her indiscretions. But one fine day the Grand Duke thought to make to Madame Pistolkors a present of some jewels which had belonged to his mother first, and to his wife afterward, and which had been locked up in a safe since the latter's death. This again might have passed unnoticed, had Madame Pistolkors not thought to put them on at a Court reception to which she was bidden. The Empress Dowager, who was present, recognized the unlucky ornaments, and, burning with wrath, forgot for once her strained relations with her daughter-in-law, and went up to her to draw her notice to the "scandal," as she termed it. Alexandra Feodorowna, as we know, had never been a tactful woman. She called a chamberlain and ordered him to invite Madame Pistolkors to leave the Palace immediately, and to escort her to her carriage. The next day Colonel Pistolkors, finding that matters had gone too far, introduced an action for divorce against his wife, and the latter, shunned by all her former friends, utterly disgraced before the world, had to flee abroad to hide her diminished head and her lost social prestige, in the solitude of a small Italian town. But then the unexpected, or rather the expected, occurred. The Grand-Duke Paul took the only course left to him compatible with his honor as a gentleman. He followed the lady to Italy and married her there without asking anybody's leave, to the general scandal of St. Petersburg society, who declared that the incident with the diamond necklace that had been the primary cause of the catastrophe had been artfully engineered by its heroine in view of the result which was ultimately achieved.

The Emperor was furious; his mother equally so, but it is not likely that anything would have been done, or in general any notice taken of the action of the Grand Duke, had it not been for the intervention of the young Empress, who insisted on her uncle-by-marriage being deprived of his rank in the army and exiled abroad. It was the first time that she had the opportunity to satisfy her instincts of hatred and of revenge in regard to a member of her husband's family, and she took a special delight, not only in doing so, but also in letting the world know that such was the case. Fate, for once kind to her, had delivered one of her enemies into her hands, and she was but too ready to seize this occasion for scoring her personal real or imaginary wrongs.

A few years later another incident of the same kind afforded her a second opportunity of exercising her powers of retaliation in regard to a Romanoff. The eldest son of the Grand-Duke Wladimir, the young Grand-Duke Cyril, the same who had nearly perished during the Japanese war in the catastrophe of the ship *Pétropawlosk*, married also without law or leave his first cousin, the divorced Grand Duchess of Hesse, the former sister-in-law of the Empress. The latter had always hated her, ever since the day that she had been obliged to play second fiddle to her at Darmstadt, and she had done her best to bring about an estrangement between her and her husband. This had not been difficult, because anything more brutal than the Grand Duke of Hesse had never existed. His young wife had had more to bear than the public knew, or that she cared herself to relate, but her own conduct had always been beyond reproach, and she had carried herself with remarkable tact and dignity. When at last she obtained her divorce, her only child, a little girl, was not even left entirely in her custody, but had to spend half of the year with the father. The latter did not well know what to do with the baby and most probably would never have availed himself of his rights had not his sister, the Empress Alexandra, interfered and persuaded him to confide to her own care the small Elisabeth, knowing very well that this would be about the most painful thing that could happen to the divorced Grand Duchess.

In accordance with this wish, the Grand Duke of Hesse brought his daughter to Spala in Poland, where the Russian Imperial Family were spending the autumn. The child sickened a few days later, and soon her condition became desperate. The doctors declared that the mother ought to be warned and asked to come, the more so that the little girl kept continually crying for her. But to this the Empress would never agree, until she knew it was positively too late. At last a telegram was sent to the Grand-Duchess Victoria Mélita; it preceded but by a few hours the one advising her that her journey would be useless, as the end had come. One may imagine the feelings of the heartbroken mother and the natural resentment she must have felt at this piece of heartlessness on the part of her former sister-in-law. For a long time she would not be comforted, but at last she was induced to listen to her cousin, the Grand-Duke Cyril, and she married him at Tegernsee in Bavaria, without the Czar's consent to this union having been so much as asked.

The rage of the Empress would be difficult to describe. Here was the sister-in-law whom she had hated for so many years the wife of a Russian Grand Duke, and of one, too, whose position put him very near to the succession to the Throne. One of those fits of hysterics to which Alexandra used to give way whenever she was crossed followed upon the news, and she insisted on the Czar declaring that he would never recognize the marriage and exiling the young couple. But here she met with an unexpected rebuff. Cyril's father, the Grand-Duke Wladimir, was still alive at the time, and he was not a man to endure any slight offered either to him or to his children. He sought the Emperor and in a stormy interview reminded the latter that his new daughter-in-law was also the granddaughter of the Czar Alexander II., and asked him what he thought the latter would have said had he seen a Princess with Romanoff blood in her veins banished from the Russian Court. Nicholas was scared, and revoked the orders he had issued a few hours before, insisting only on the newly married pair not coming back to Russia for a few months, after which he left them free to do what they liked.

Alexandra Feodorowna was defeated, and this did not improve by any means her temper nor her feelings in regard to the Imperial Family. She then bethought herself to win over to her side that same Grand-Duke Paul against whom she had been so incensed at the time he had married Madame Fistolkors. It must here be added that one of the reasons for her change of opinion in that respect lay in the fact that she had by that time struck up the extraordinary intimacy with Madame Wyrubewa which was to have such sinister consequences later on, and that this lady had always been one of the closest friends of the morganatic wife of Paul Alexandrowitch. The latter was therefore invited to return to Russia and given to understand that it depended on him to be reinstated in favor, if only he would take the Empress's part against their other relatives. Of course he promised he would do so, and we shall see presently what resulted of this intrigue in the years which followed.

Cyril and his wife returned to Tsarskoye Selo and to St. Petersburg in due course. They were received by both the Czar and Czarina coldly but civilly. Alexandra, however, persisted in her determination to keep her former sister-in-law at arm's-length, and the relations between the two ladies remained official, without the least attempt at any intimacy, until the Revolution sent the Empress into exile and threw into the arms of its leaders both Cyril Wladimirowitch and Victoria Mélita.

It was known already at the time that one of the persons who had the most contributed to excite Alexandra Feodorowna against her cousins had been Madame Wyrubewa. The latter was a new importation at Court, who, thanks to a very clever piece of strategy, had won the good graces of the Empress, whom she had met under rather peculiar circumstances. She was the daughter of a certain Mr. Tanieiew, who occupied important official functions at Court, and she had contrived to let the Czarina hear, through her father, that she was engaged in the occupation of writing a history of Hesse, which she meant to present to a public-school library or other institution of the same kind. Alexandra was immediately interested and asked to see the work. She sent for Madame Wyrubewa and soon the latter became her friend and confidante.

Madame Wyrubewa knew very well what she was about, even before circumstances turned out favorably in regard to her views and designs. She fully meant to become the Gray Eminence of the Empress, and, like the famous Père Joseph of Richelieu, to rule her, and through her the whole of Russia. We shall presently see how she proceeded to reach her aim, which in the mean while she knew very well she could never attain so long as there were near the Czar people whose close relationship with him allowed them to speak quite frankly with him on all subjects, even on that of the caprices and extraordinary behavior of his wife.

Anna Wyrubewa contrived to create a deadly feud between the Imperial pair and the whole clan of the Grand-Duke Wladimir's family, who in a certain way was most powerful. The other members of the family were not dangerous in so far that the only thing they aspired to was to be left severely alone, and that they never cared to trouble with their presence the Emperor and Empress, for whom their dislike was only equaled by their contempt. There was only to be feared the Grand-Duke Michael, the only brother of Nicholas II. and his Heir so long as the Empress had not given birth to a son. It was therefore against him that the new favorite turned her attention and against him that she excited the revengeful feelings of Alexandra Feodorowna.

What I wish to point out at present is that one of the secrets of the extraordinary influence which Anna Wyrubewa acquired over the mind of her Imperial mistress lay in the extreme ability which she displayed in appealing to all the bad sentiments of the latter, under the pretext of pitying her, and condoling with her on all the real or imaginary troubles of her life. She soon made herself indispensable to the Sovereign, who liked to visit her in her house, where she knew that no one would interfere with her and where she could meet the few people with whom she thoroughly sympathized, who in their turn were but too glad to have an opportunity of seeing almost in tête-à-tête the otherwise unapproachable Empress of Russia.

The small drawing-room full of flowers, where Alexandra Feodorowna was to spend so many happy and peaceful hours, and which was to witness in time such memorable events, filled itself with all manner of people, who, by common accord, never spoke of having been admitted within its precincts, or of having met one another there. It became also the meeting-place of a party, small at first, important later on; not, perhaps, on account of its number, but by the character of those who constituted it; a party that came to be known by the name of the "Empress's Party." It was to number among its adherents men like Mr. Sturmer, the latter's secretary, the too-famous Manassavitch-Maniuloff, Mr. Protopopoff, and, last but not least, the vagrant preacher who for a short time was to be the dominant figure in Russian politics, Grigory Raspoutine.

CHAPTER XI

AND HE SAW HER PASS . . .

MADAME WYRUBEWA was a very clever woman, and an ambitious one into the bargain. Her ambition, however, was absolutely different from what might have been expected of a person brought up in the atmosphere of a Court and having been, if not actually mixed up, at least well posted, thanks to the position occupied by her father and family. She knew all the intrigues which always flourished and made the Court of St. Petersburg such a slippery ground for those who did not possess sufficient support to hold their own amid the rivalries and gossip which constituted the daily existence of the Imperial Family and of their friends. She did not care in the least for money, having got enough for her wants, nor for rank or position, which she knew too well could be lost or obtained according to circumstances, and which, besides, were never sufficient in Russia to make or mar an individual whose social worth depended only on the manner in which he was viewed by the Sovereign—the words of Paul I., when he said that the only persons deserving of any notice in his Empire were those "to whom he spoke, and only while he spoke with them." These words, about which one had laughed all through the three preceding reigns, had come to be absolutely true during that of Nicholas II., when favoritism assumed hitherto unknown proportions, as none knew better than Anna Wyrubewa, whose quick wit and ever-alert intelligence discovered very soon that she would become a far more important personage if she remained in the background content with being the Empress's friend, if she did not work toward obtaining for herself or for her husband a Court appointment or a lucrative official post. She aspired to something much more tangible, and at the same time much more amusing. She wanted to rule the Empress, and through her the whole of the vast Russian Empire. This young and delicate woman had the head of a statesman, and she might have risen to unheard-of might if she had not allowed those superstitious leanings which are inherent in the Russian character in so many cases to get the upper hand of her reason and lead her, together with her Imperial mistress, into the manifold mistakes which culminated in the catastrophe that destroyed the Throne of the Romanoffs.

At the same time Madame Wyrubewa sincerely loved the Empress. About this there is no doubt. She began by feeling sorry for the sad, miserable woman, so lonely amid her luxury and splendor, who stood friendless and defenseless among implacable enemies. She did not stop to consider whether this situation had arisen out of the personal fault of Alexandra Feodorowna, or out of other circumstances. She simply saw the fact, and hearing, as she did, all the different rumors concerning the Czarina which were going about in St. Petersburg society, she conceived the idea of coming to her help, and trying to be to her that friend in need she had never found since she came to Russia in quest of a Crown. This latter had certainly turned out to be, for her, one of thorns!

When her relations with the unfortunate Sovereign in whose life she was to play such an important part began, Anna Wyrubewa did not look beyond this simple fact, finding out how she could best be useful to her. The whole of St. Petersburg was discussing the question of a possible divorce which would send Alexandra Feodorowna into a convent, and bets had been made in select circles of Court society as to whether or not this would really take place. It was known that her relations with the Emperor were anything but tender, and that numerous quarrels had taken place between them.

Nicholas II., after an interval of several years, had resumed his former relations with Mademoiselle Krzesinska, and the dancer was contributing perhaps more than she herself suspected to sow dissension in the Imperial *ménage*. The Empress, as we know, was exceedingly proud, and as soon as she perceived, which did not take very long, that her husband was seeking amusement outside his home, she retired once more in haughty silence into the solitude of her own apartments and refused to fulfil the social duties required from her by her position, to the disgust of her friends and the joy of her numerous enemies. Matters had got to such a pass that sometimes days used to go by without the Czar and Czarina exchanging one single word beyond what was absolutely necessary during meals, and even these were not always taken together, Alexandra Feodorowna often putting forward her health as an excuse for having her dinner or lunch served in her own apartments. She was simply playing into her enemies' hands, and, whether consciously or unconsciously, herself tightening around her neck the rope which had been put within her reach.

It was this that made Anna Wyrubewa determined to come to the help of the unfortunate Sovereign whom she saw going with rapid steps toward ultimate destruction. She tried to reason with her, to speak to her of the necessity of not giving up the game, and of her imperative duty to remain upon good terms with her husband, so as to be able to bear him the son whose absence contributed so much to the bad relations that had taken the place of the affectionate ones which had undoubtedly existed at one time between her and Nicholas II. But the Empress would not listen, declaring that she was tired of always giving birth to girls, whose advent into the world only added to her unhappiness, and that, besides, she was sick of a husband whose deplorable weakness of character made him an easy prey for the first intriguing person who approached him. The only thing which she wished was to return to Darmstadt, together with her daughters; but as she knew very well that she would never be allowed to take them out of Russia, she preferred to be sent to a convent, where she could end her days in prayer, and where she could bring up her children without any interference from the outside world. The Emperor could divorce her and marry again; she did not care; all she wished for was a quiet life, far from those detestable Court intrigues that had wrecked all the hopes of happiness she had ever had.

Anna Wyrubewa listened, and very gently applied herself to reason with the sorely tried woman. She told her that it would be unworthy to throw up the game, but, on the contrary, that her duty toward her daughters required her to fight vigorously against destiny represented by the Empress Dowager, the Grand Dukes, the Court, and the nation, who judged her according to what it had been told of her. She repeated to her that if once she had a son her position would change immediately, and the affection of her husband would return to her, together with the popularity she had lost in the country. Alexandra only replied by floods of tears and complaints that she did not know how such a desirable event could happen. She loathed the Emperor and she knew that he did not care for her; that, in fact, no one cared for her; and that was the calamity which to her sensitive heart appeared the most terrible one among all those that had befallen her.

Madame Wyrubewa was at her wits' end, but she did not despair. She felt, however, that she could not cope alone with the many difficulties which she found in her way, and so she looked round her to see whether she could not find any one in whom she could confide, and from whom she might, in her turn, seek advice.

I don't know whether I have related that the lady had always been a favorite in society. At that time she was going out a great deal, which was not the case later on, when her whole position changed and when she became the Empress's principal confidante, and had perforce to live in retirement. But twelve or fifteen years ago her house in Tsarskoye Selo was the meeting-place of a select circle, and especially of the officers of the regiments constituting the garrison of the Imperial Residence, who liked to drop in of an evening, and find a pleasant hostess, together with an excellent supper which was always waiting for them. Mr. Wyrubew, too, was a general favorite, and altogether the little house occupied by the young couple was very popular with the inhabitants of the Imperial Borough.

Among the special friends of Anna Wyrubewa was a dashing officer called Colonel Orloff. He had a commission in the regiment of Lancers of the Guard, the chief of whom was the Empress Alexandra. A wonderfully handsome man, he was also clever, brave, chivalrous, and altogether different from his comrades in so far that he had never cared for the boisterous pleasures which made up their daily existence. One day as he was going to call on Madame Wyrubewa he saw the Czarina leave her house in a state of evident agitation. Alexandra was alone and on foot, having walked from the Palace to her friend's house, and the Colonel, who, on recognizing the Sovereign, had respectfully stood aside, was much surprised to notice her red eyes and her general attitude of dejection. He waited until she had disappeared among the trees in the park and then rang the door-bell of Madame Wyrubewa.

He found her just as agitated as the Empress, and when he asked her what was the matter he was much surprised to see her begin to weep.

She related to him that she was terribly anxious about the fate of the unlucky Consort of Nicholas II., whose safety and person were threatened as much by her own stupidity as by the intrigues of her numerous enemies. Colonel Orloff listened in silence. He, too, was troubled by this unexpected revelation; the more so that for years he had nourished a secret adoration and worship for Alexandra Feodorowna, which he had hoped no one had, or would ever discover, and the news of her danger was terrible for him. His emotion was so evident that Anna noticed it at once, and an idea which was yet vague and misty began to take shape in her active brain, and induced her to seek the help of this unexpected ally whom circumstances and accident had brought to her. She started to discuss the situation seriously with the young officer, and together they determined to try and save the Empress, even against her own will, from the snares into which she was walking with an unconsciousness which was almost too pitiful to look upon otherwise than with a wild desire to snatch her away from the abyss whither she was sinking with what promised to become rapidity.

Colonel Orloff had a wonderful talent for music. On the very next day following upon the conversation which I have related, Madame Wyrubewa asked him to call on her in the afternoon, and to perform for her some melodies of Chopin which she knew were the favorite ones of the Empress. She also begged the latter to allow the Colonel to play for them, saying that it might interest her to hear him. Alexandra consented and, as in the case of David and Saul, she found a solace in listening to the wonderful music. Very soon she got into the habit of dropping in at her friend's whenever she had a spare moment, and then Orloff would be telephoned for, and he used to come and hold the two ladies under the spell of his rare talent. Of course no one was admitted to these meetings and no one knew anything about them. At that time people did not trouble about the Empress of All the Russias, and her actions did not offer the slightest interest to any one, to the Emperor least of all.

Colonel Orloff was something in character like the famous Count Fersen, the admirer and devoted friend of Marie Antoinette. He, too, had conceived a passion for his Sovereign, in whom he only saw the unfortunate, ill-treated, and misunderstood woman, and he conceived the thought to sacrifice everything for her service, to try and save her from the perils with which he saw her surrounded. And gradually, when his relations with her became more real and intimate, he, too, began to speak to her in the same sense as Anna Wyrubewa had done, of the necessity of trying to reconcile herself with her husband so as to be able to bring into the world that Heir after whom the whole of Russia had been longing for the last nine years or so.

One day Madame Wyrubewa, whether accidentally or intentionally, left the Colonel alone with the Czarina. He saw his opportunity, and began more seriously than he had ever done before to implore her to make an effort to save herself. The young man grew quite eloquent, until Alexandra, moved beyond words, started weeping in real earnest and asked him how he could suggest the possibility of a reconciliation between her and the Czar, in view of his own feelings for her, the nature of which she had guessed for some time. To her surprise, the Colonel fell on his knees before her and told her that it was because of these very feelings that he had felt himself justified in speaking to her as he had done. He was nothing beside her, and all he could do was to worship her from afar, and to try to come to her help, both for her own sake and for that of their country, that required from them both the supreme sacrifice he was asking of her. For once the cold and haughty Czarina was startled out of her usual indifference, and when they parted she had promised her devoted knight and admirer that, though she might not make an effort to win back the love of her husband, yet she would not repulse him, as she had done lately, if he made any attempt to return to her. She promised that on the love she owned to him that she felt for him, and on that of the one which they both had for this great Russia, which Orloff had never forgotten even amid the fervor of his passion. When Madame Wyrubewa came back to the room where she had left her two friends, she saw that something had happened, but she was far too clever to question them, and when the Empress said it was time for her to go home she simply offered to accompany her, hoping that something might be told to her during their walk back to the Palace. For once Alexandra was silent, and parted from Anna without betraying anything of what had passed during that half-hour when she had been left alone with the first man who had aroused some interest in her otherwise impassible heart.

Colonel Orloff was not so discreet, in the sense that he related to his friend all that had taken place between him and the Czarina—related it with such agitation and poignant regret that she saw at once that she was in the presence of a feeling capable of driving the man who was under its influence to any heights of personal sacrifice. She then communicated to him a plan out of which she hoped to find the solution of the troubles against which the Empress was struggling so bravely, but apparently so uselessly. It was a daring plan and it required much daring to accomplish it; but the future of the woman they both loved was at stake, and she thought they ought to risk it.

Nicholas II. was fond of Colonel Orloff, whom he had recently appointed one of his aides-de-camp. The Sovereign liked from time to time to go and dine or have supper at the mess of some regiment or other of the Guards, either at Tsarskoye Selo, Peterhof, or St. Petersburg. These entertainments used to last generally into the small hours of the morning, and ill-natured people said that the Czar when in this company of young men, which was more congenial to him than the one he was compelled to see generally, allowed himself to have more glasses of wine than were good for him, and to indulge in subjects of conversation he would have done better to avoid. Whether this was true or not, it is of course difficult to say, but the fact remains that Nicholas liked these "family festivities," as he used to call them, and that he always returned home in a good temper after having attended them. Colonel Orloff was aware of this weakness of the Sovereign, and one day he proposed to him to go and hear some regimental singers at the mess of his own Lancer regiment, stationed at Peterhof, the same regiment of which the Empress was Colonel-in-chief. Nicholas II. consented and a day was fixed. On the morning of that day Colonel Orloff sought Madame Wyrubewa; the two had a long conversation, the result of which was their reading together a certain page in French history relating how Louis XIII. had been compelled to seek the hospitality of his wife, Anne of Austria, on a stormy night when it had not been possible for him to return from Paris to St.-Germain, where he resided, an incident that had had world-wide consequences in the birth of the child who was to become in time Louis XIV. After that the Colonel returned to the Palace, where he was on duty that day, and his friend went to seek the Empress and to try to induce her to lend a helping hand to the plot which they had both engineered.

The supper took place, and it was nearly dawn when the Czar left the mess of the Lancers of the Guard, where he declared that he had spent a most pleasant evening. He drove in a motor-car back to Tsarskoye Selo in a very enjoyable frame of mind, which did not require the encouragement of his aide-de-camp, who sat next to him, to become a boisterous one. Lots of champagne had been drunk during the meal, and even after, and when some one in the gay assembly had ventured to say that the only pity of the whole thing was that no representatives of the fair sex had been invited to enliven the party with their presence, Nicholas II. had heartily echoed the regret expressed by the officer in question. Orloff, when alone with the Sovereign, had very cleverly turned the conversation into the same channel, and at last had wormed out of his Imperial Master the confession that he was very unhappy at the extreme coldness of character of his Consort, whose beauty he admired just as much as on the day he had married her. The Colonel, upon this, had ventured to express the conviction that this coldness was only assumed, and proceeded perhaps from jealousy more than from anything else. When at last Tsarskoye Selo was reached, instead of accompanying Nicholas to his own apartments, as it was part of his duties to do, he brought him to the door of the Empress's room, which he opened and closed upon him.

The next day a pale and haggard woman appeared in Anna Wyrubewa's house, coming to seek consolation in what she considered an overwhelming misfortune, and while she was sobbing out the agony of her soul with her head hidden in her friend's lap, a strong man who had borne many a misfortune without flinching, and who had stood calm and unmoved while his heart had been breaking, was sitting alone in his room, his head hidden in his hands, and hot tears dropping one by one between his fingers on the table over which he was leaning, in his overwhelming despair.

CHAPTER XII

LOVED AT LAST

AFTER a storm there comes, generally, so they say, at least, a great calm. And in a certain sense this happened in regard to the troubled mind of the Empress Alexandra. As time went on, she recognized the value of the good advice which she had received from Madame Wyrubewa as well as from Colonel Orloff. Her relations with the Czar, which had been more than strained for long months, became gradually better when she could at last tell him that she had once again, and this time without any mistake, the hope of giving him the Heir for which they had been longing. She saw his former confidence in her return, together with his affection; an affection to which she did not perhaps respond, but which she nevertheless appreciated, perhaps because she was told she ought to do so.

The fact was that her two friends were doing their best to get her to take a healthier view of her own position than had been the case until then. Intrigues at the Court were getting worse and worse, as the various events which finally brought about the Japanese war were slowly unfolding themselves, and it became every day more important for the security of the Empress that she should not disinterest herself from all that was going on around her, as had been her wont, since she had allowed disappointment and sorrow to overpower her.

It was an anxious and a critical time for the dynasty as well as for the country that was coming on, and Anna Wyrubewa with her clear mind was very well aware that such was the case. She used to hear all the gossip in the various circles of St. Petersburg society, and she knew very well that a war was wished for by the enemies of the existing order of things. They saw in it the possibility of overthrowing the dynasty, as the mistakes inevitable in dealing with such a corrupt administration as the Russian one would appear in a new, bold light before the horrified eyes of the public. She was also perfectly aware of the growing unpopularity of Nicholas II., and of the way in which he was daily losing what still remained of the former short-lived affection his subjects had felt for him. She would have liked the Empress to assert herself, and to claim as her right to be initiated in what was going on in the domain of public affairs, but it was still too early for Alexandra to avail herself of this advice. The Czarina did not feel sure of her ground as yet, and she only replied to her friend's adjurations that, if she were lucky enough to give birth to a son, she would follow her advice to the letter; in the mean while she felt afraid of being snubbed by the Emperor, who, though he treated her with far more consideration than he had done for a long time, still kept her in total ignorance of all questions relating to the affairs of the State. On the other hand, he did not hesitate to discuss them with his mother, the Dowager Empress, and even occasionally with his sisters and his brother-in-law, the Grand-Duke Alexander Michaylovitch, who had always been his great friend and favorite.

The delicate condition of health of Alexandra Feodorowna furnished her with the pretext she required to isolate herself more than ever from her family, and she used to spend long hours with Madame Wyrubewa in the latter's small house, and whenever she went there she met, as if accidentally, Colonel Orloff, whose faithful, devoted eyes followed her with a love which she could not have helped noticing, even if she had not been aware of its existence. She was a woman gifted with a very pure mind, given to idealize the people she cared for and her own feelings in regard to them. She soon grew to think of the young officer as of a kind of guardian angel sent by Providence to help her in the various difficulties of her daily existence, and with a selfishness almost touching in its unconsciousness she took to confiding to him her various doubts and perplexities, and to initiate him into all the details of her married life, together with the constant disgust and struggles which attended it, not suspecting that by doing so she was breaking the heart of this one faithful friend who had sacrificed himself so entirely to her welfare.

In the mean while events had been rapidly unfolding themselves. The war with Japan had begun and was progressing, together with its long series of appalling disasters coming one on top of the other. Mukden had been fought, the *Pétropawlosk* had gone down in the waves of the Pacific, with brave Admiral Makharoff and its whole crew of officers and men, and the catastrophe of Tsu Shima had also taken place. These had been met by the utter indifference of Nicholas II., who had not even thought it worth while to interrupt the game of tennis he had been playing when the telegram with the news of this unprecedented misfortune had been brought to him. In the interior of the country trouble was also brewing. The Grand-Duke Sergius, the uncle of the Czar and the husband of the Empress's eldest sister, Elisabeth, had fallen under the bomb of an assassin in Moscow, and the famous Minister of the Interior, Von Plehwe, whose very name was a horror to all the liberal elements in the land, had met with the same fate.

It was evident that grave events were at hand, and that unless something was attempted to meet them the very foundations of the Throne might come to be shaken by this rising tide of discontent which threatened to engulf the dynasty in its waves. It was high time something were done, and that some one should interfere to save Nicholas II. from impending calamity. Who could do so better than his wife and the mother of his children? Thus reasoned Anna Wyrubewa, and it was also what her friend, Colonel Orloff, thought; but that was not at all what was wished by the various other forces at work trying to dictate to the weak-minded Czar the conduct he ought to hold in the presence of these unexpected difficulties with which he found himself confronted, to his dismay and surprise. There had got about among the public an inkling as to the possibility of the Empress becoming all at once a factor to be reckoned with in the general situation. Immediately the efforts of all her enemies became concentrated on that one point—how best to eliminate this new element, which they understood but too well would necessarily counteract their own influence.

A careful watch was set on the person and the conduct of the young Sovereign. It did not bring any of the hoped-for results, because both Anna Wyrubewa and Colonel Orloff were prudent people, who contrived to arrange matters in such a way, that no one suspected they used to see Alexandra Feodorowna every day, and who had persuaded the latter to resort to all kinds of precautions whenever she visited her friend.

One day, however, an officer who was serving in that very same regiment of Lancers to which Colonel Orloff belonged made a playful remark to the effect that he was believed to be a favorite with the lovely and cold Czarina, who had never hitherto allowed her glances to fall on any man whatsoever. The young Colonel became immediately alarmed, the more so that he could not discover the source whence this piece of gossip had arisen. He sought Madame Wyrubewa and told her that he had made up his mind to ask to be transferred to a regiment at the front, so as to put a quick end to any possible unpleasantness. She heartily agreed with him in the opinion that this was the best thing he could do, for the sake of everybody, and especially for that of the Empress.

The latter had to be told of Orloff's resolution. But when he broke to her his intention to request the favor of risking his life in distant Manchuria, she gave way to a fit of despair that absolutely frightened her two devoted friends, and implored him not to leave her, at least not until her child had been born, saying with sobs and tears that she would never be able to undergo the trial which awaited her if she did not know that he was there, as near to her as possible, and that she could see him after all was over, to wish her joy, if the expected babe were a son, and to comfort her if it turned out to be another girl, the one thing which she feared above all others.

At first the Colonel protested. He tried to explain to the despairing and over-excited woman that it was for her sake he wished to go away, at least for a while, and that it cost him more than he could say to come to such a resolution, but that he loved her far too much to let her run any risk. The Empress would not listen to anything, and at last she told him that if he went away she would consider it as a proof that he did not love her, and that all he had said to her had been nothing but empty phrases, such as no doubt he had repeated already to many more women than he even cared to remember. Orloff was stung to the quick, but he remained, nevertheless, firm until Alexandra Feodorowna exclaimed that unless he promised her to remain by her side she would make a scandal and depart for Darmstadt, whether the Emperor allowed her to do so or not. Man-like, he yielded, without suspecting whither this weakness was to lead him sooner than he could imagine.

While this drama was going on in the pretty little house whither Anna Wyrubewa received the Empress of All the Russias, unknown to the rest of the world, so she believed, at least, speculations were rife as to the eventual sex of the child expected by the Czar and Czarina. Everybody, with few exceptions, hoped that it would be another daughter, none more ardently than the Dowager Empress, who would have infinitely preferred the Throne passing to her youngest son than to any boy born to a daughter-in-law whom she made no secret of disliking, and whom she distrusted even more than she disliked. She realized very well that Alexandra Feodorowna, if she was the mother of an Heir to the Imperial Crown, would become a most important personage in the State, as well as in the eyes of her husband. This was not to be desired, in view of her strong German sympathies, which she had lately exhibited more than she had ever dared to do before.

The French alliance was very popular at the time I am talking about, and the Empress was considered as its principal and most bitter adversary. This was one more reason for not wishing her to acquire suddenly an importance that had never been awarded to her by the nation since she had become its Sovereign.

For months this kind of thing went on. Alexandra Feodorowna knew herself to be watched with anything but kind eyes, and this consciousness of the ill-will of which she was the object added to her anxiety and moral sufferings. As the weary months dragged on, she thought more and more of Orloff, and suddenly she realized that she loved him more than any one in the world, and she began to understand all that she must have cost him, in pain and vain regret.

But for her, at least, consolation was at hand. One July morning the Imperial Family were called together with the principal Court and State functionaries in all haste to Peterhof. The long-expected event was at hand, and a few hours would decide as to the future of the Romanoff dynasty. People with anxious faces thronged the vast halls of the Palace, waiting for news which seemed to be very long in coming.

At last, just as the clock struck noon, a doctor entered the room, and told the assistants that Nicholas II. was the father of a son.

There was one person present who listened to this announcement with an impassible face but with a breaking heart, and who could barely find sufficient strength to reach the little cottage where Anna Wyrubewa was sitting pale and anxious, in expectation of—she did not know well herself what. When she saw Colonel Orloff she extended toward him her two hands in a gesture of passionate greeting. But what was her surprise to see him fall on the sofa beside her and bury his head in the silk cushions, with such sobs as rarely shake the frame of a strong man. He had had the courage to sacrifice his personal happiness at the shrine of the woman whom he adored with such religious fervor, but it was more than he could bear to find how thoroughly this sacrifice had been accepted by Providence, and for just a few minutes he had hated this new-born child, whom he knew but too well was going to usurp the place he had hoped to keep forever in the heart and the affections of Alexandra Feodorowna.

CHAPTER XIII

HE DIED TO SAVE HER HONOR

THE christening of the little Grand-Duke Alexis was solemnized with great pomp at Peterhof, and there is no doubt but that the position of his mother became, after his birth, quite different from what it had been before this much-wished-for baby had appeared. For one thing, the talk of a divorce between her and the Czar, which had been so frequently indulged in, came to an end, and it was felt, even by the most bitter enemies of the Empress, that it would be waste of time to think about the possibility of its ever taking place.

Nicholas II., in his joy at having at last an Heir, seemed to have returned to his former allegiance in regard to his wife, and he began to confide in her far more than he had done formerly, even consulting her on different occasions. She was the mother of the future Sovereign, and as such entitled to a consideration a childless Empress Dowager could never aspire to in the case of widowhood. It became, therefore, necessary to initiate her in matters concerning the government of the country, and the Czar did this the more willingly that at heart he distrusted his brother, and his numerous uncles and cousins, and feared that in case he died before the small Cesarewitsch had reached his majority the interests of the latter would not be looked after as well as would be necessary, unless his mother were there to protect them.

Alexandra Feodorowna, on the other hand, urged by her two friends, Madame Wyrubewa and Colonel Orloff, began to show far more interest in public affairs than she had ever done since her marriage, and she tried to establish between herself and her husband more intimate relations than she had cared to do formerly, when she used to spend her days lamenting over sorrows, imaginary most of the time, but sufficiently acute to render her intensely miserable. Her son became the principal preoccupation of her existence, and she would not intrust his care to any one, but transformed herself into his nurse, governess, and constant attendant, forgetting everything else, even the care of her daughters, in her nervous solicitude for him. Unfortunately the child was born excessively delicate, and had a curious and rare disease, a weakness of the blood-vessels, which were affected in such a way that he was attacked with hemorrhage at the slightest touch; the smallest of knocks or wounds would endanger his life. He might bleed to death from an ordinary bruise. An unfortunate accident which occurred when he was two years old, and which brought about a rupture that necessitated an operation from which he recovered only by a kind of miracle, only aggravated the chronic ailment with which he was afflicted.

One may imagine how terrible this state of things proved for the Empress, who very stupidly, as it seemed to some people, applied herself to hide from the public the state of physical health of her son, which had, among other results, that of people supposing him to be even more dangerously ill than was the case. The truth was that Alexandra feared that if it were known the boy was afflicted with an incurable disease, it might add to her own unpopularity. Her friends hoped that she might bear another son in time, but after the birth of Alexis she never had any more hopes of maternity, and so there remained nothing else to do but to try and rear this weak, frail, and puny infant, in whom were centered all the future hopes of the proud Romanoff dynasty.

Anna Wyrubewa did her best to comfort the sorrowing mother, and both she and Colonel Orloff agreed that the only thing to do in order to turn her thoughts into another channel than that of her child's state of health, over which she brooded until she had become absolutely morbid in her constant preoccupation of the painful subject, was to speak to her of the necessity of becoming the Czar's principal adviser and counselor. They tried to induce her to assert herself in the interest of Alexis, who they assured her would one day outgrow his native weakness and require her help in the numerous duties entailed upon him by his position as Heir to the Throne. In a certain sense they succeeded, and the Empress began to develop an independence of opinions and views in which she had never dared to indulge before. Ministers were surprised to hear the Czar say to them, when they pressed him for a reply to some decision or order they presented to him for confirmation, that he first wished to discuss the subject with his wife. Somehow there arose among the public, and especially among the Imperial Family, an impression that Alexandra had at last completely subjugated her husband, and that she was henceforward a factor to be reckoned with in every important State affair which might arise in regard to foreign or home politics.

Of course people did not like it. One had been used for such a long time to consider the Czarina as a nonentity that it seemed a strange thing to have suddenly to take her into account; one began to wonder what could have brought about such an unexpected change in her whole conduct and demeanor. Maternal love was not sufficient to explain it, and the cause of it had to be looked for elsewhere, and one fine day her constant intercourse with Anna Wyrubewa was noticed. Once people were started on that path, there was but one step to take—to try and find out whether or not these suspicions were founded on anything tangible. Some inquisitive persons took to watching the actions of Anna Wyrubewa, and they were not long in discovering that her house served as a meeting-place for several people in whom Alexandra Feodorowna was interested, among others Colonel Orloff, whose hopeless passion for his Sovereign had been already suspected at different times.

Foremost among these voluntary observators, not to give them another name, figured members of the Imperial Family who had never taken kindly to the Consort of Nicholas II., and who hated the idea of her becoming a power in the State. They tried to find out something to her detriment, and who also attempted to enroll among their number the Dowager-Empress Marie, who, however, refused to listen to them, and whose affection for her eldest son induced her to make an effort to warn her daughter-in-law of the dangers which were threatening her. But the young Czarina would not hear anything, and haughtily refused the hand that was extended to her in sincere friendship. She snubbed Marie Feodorowna in such a manner that the latter, wounded to the quick in finding her good intentions misunderstood, swore that she would never again attempt to come to the help of a person who was so prejudiced against her.

In the mean while, ignorant of the conspiracy which was being engineered against her, Alexandra continued to spend her afternoons with Madame Wyrubewa, often taking her little boy with her. The two women watched the child sleeping in his cradle, and often Colonel Orloff shared their vigil with a bleeding heart, the baby reminding him of all that he had suffered for the sake of its mother, but with the consciousness of having done his duty to both. But one day rumors again reached his ears that his name had once more become associated with that of the Empress. This time he made up his mind to go away definitely, no matter how much she might ask him to stay. He realized, if neither she nor Anna Wyrubewa did so, that the position was becoming threatening, and that he ought to put an end to it in some way or other. Unfortunately, when he came to this conclusion it was already too late.

Madame Wyrubewa's husband was a naval officer, not gifted with a superabundance of brains, but honest in his way, and incapable of intrigues of any kind. He had troubled very little about his wife, and was perhaps the only man in St. Petersburg and in Tsarskoye Selo who was not aware of the high favor in which she stood with the Empress. His duties generally kept him far from his home most of the year, and when he was there he rarely troubled Anna with his presence. But he was known to be of a violent disposition, and as a fellow who would not suffer any stain to rest upon his honor. It was of this man that the enemies of Alexandra Feodorowna determined to make use in order to ruin her.

Anonymous letters were sent to him accusing his wife of carrying on a guilty intrigue with Colonel Orloff, intrigue which he was assured the Empress knew and favored. He was advised to return home unexpectedly any afternoon between four and five o'clock, when he would find proofs of the information vouchsafed to him by his unknown friend. The young man, instead of putting these denunciations in the fire, became so enraged that he determined to follow the advice of his anonymous correspondent. After having advised Anna that he was going away on a few days' cruise, he waited until the hour that had been indicated to him, and boldly walked back to his house.

He was met at the door by the Cossack in personal attendance on the Empress, who informed him that he could not get in. Wyrubew protested, and was quietly told that the Sovereign was visiting his wife, and that according to etiquette no one could be allowed to enter a place where she was unless by her special permission. The officer became furious, brushed the Cossack aside, and penetrated into the sitting-room, after having noticed that a military overcoat was hanging in his hall. He found the apartment empty, but in the adjoining one, which was Anna's boudoir, he could hear voices, one of which was distinctly masculine. He did not hesitate, but made his way inside, to find that his wife was not there, but that the Empress, pale and lovely, was standing by the mantelpiece, while Colonel Orloff, on his knees before her, was kissing passionately the hem of her skirt.

Alexandra Feodorowna gave one cry, which echoed through the whole building and brought Madame Wyrubewa to her help. Wyrubew himself remained silent and dazed by the unexpected sight. The only one not to lose presence of mind was Colonel Orloff, who, starting to his feet, went up to the intruder with the stern words:

"You are going to give me your word of honor to remain silent."

Wyrubew passed his hand over his eyes. He could hardly believe his own senses, and the terrible idea crossed his mind that his wife had been helping the Czarina in an amorous intrigue, and that very probably he would have to pay the penalty for this piece of complaisance, which he did not in the least care to do. He thought that insolence was the best way to get out of an impossible position with flying colors, and so he simply sneered in the face of Orloff, with the remark:

"Not I. If you have chosen to abuse my confidence, together with my wife, you cannot expect me to help you in your villainy."

Anna rushed to the Empress and took her in her arms, trying to lead her out of the room. Orloff made a movement forward as if he wanted to strangle Wyrubew; then he contained himself and said in a low voice:

"You know that you are not speaking the truth. Once more I implore you not to mention to any one what has taken place here, and I give you my word of honor to meet you whenever and wherever you like."

"You are not a man from whom one can expect satisfaction," replied Wyrubew, "and I will not claim it from you. There are other means at my disposal to punish you," and he turned away contemptuously.

The young Colonel's face became by turns deadly pale and fiery red. It was evident that he could hardly contain the tumultuous feelings which were racking him. Before him stood the Czarina looking at him with haggard eyes and trying to free herself from the encircling arms of her friend. Anna was weeping profusely and vainly struggling with an emotion she absolutely could not control. Orloff went up to the two women, and once more knelt before the Empress.

"Forgive me," he said. "I ought to have known better, but believe me, I shall atone."

He kissed once more the hem of her garment and went out of the room, without looking round, brushing past Wyrubew as if he had not seen him, and went back to his own house, calm and determined, but probably with the feelings of a man about to be taken to the scaffold.

Madame Wyrubewa seized her husband by the arm.

"Go now," she cried. "You have done enough evil for to-day, but remember that henceforth everything is at end between us."

He laughed sardonically, but obeyed her, and the couple never set eyes upon each other again after that terrible afternoon. The next day St. Petersburg was electrified by hearing that the popular Colonel Orloff had been found dead in his room, shot through the temple. He had atoned.

And two months later the Synod pronounced the decree of divorce between Anna Wyrubewa and her husband. The tragedy, like so many others of the same kind, had come to an end, by breaking two women's hearts.

CHAPTER XIV

A NATION IN REVOLT

THE suicide of Colonel Orloff was perhaps one of the events which provoked the most sensation in St. Petersburg in recent years. Everybody had known him, and he had been a general favorite, not only in his regiment, but also among all the circles of society which he had frequented. The Czar, who had also liked him very much, was deeply affected by the catastrophe, and everybody kept wondering what could have induced a man who apparently had not a single thing in the world to trouble him to take his own life in such an unexpected manner.

The Empress alone said nothing. She was present at all the funeral services which were celebrated over the coffin of the young officer, but so was Nicholas II. Her attendance could not be considered as an extraordinary thing. No one, with the exception of Anna Wyrubewa, who had accompanied her, knew that on the night preceding the funeral of her friend Alexandra Feodorowna had proceeded alone and unattended, save for her, to the house where his mortal remains lay in state, and had spent an hour praying beside his dead body and weeping bitter tears. Outwardly, however, her calm had remained unshaken; and she had succeeded in quite a wonderful way in keeping her feelings under control. The only thing which she had insisted upon was to have Colonel Orloff buried in the cemetery of Tsarskoye Selo, where she had a simple monument, consisting of a large white marble cross, erected. She used to go every day to pray there, and to leave flowers on this tomb which represented for her so many hopes, and perhaps something else besides.

Of course these visits became known, but by a wonderful miracle they were not commented upon in the way they might have been. The reputation for eccentricity of Alexandra Feodorowna had by that time become so well established that people had left off wondering at anything she might attempt to do, and, besides, every one believed that the Colonel's death had been somehow connected with a love intrigue he had carried on with Anna Wyrubewa, whose divorce lent ground for such a theory. It was suspected or guessed that something had taken place in her house, but no one could exactly ascertain what this something had been, and Wyrubew himself had been for once thoroughly frightened, and had come to the conclusion that the best thing he could do for his own sake as well as for that of others was to hold his tongue, and to accept the divorce upon which his wife insisted. Later on, however, he unburdened his soul to some of his particular friends, but that happened at a time when people were thinking of other things than the tragical death of an officer whose existence was already forgotten by most of those who had known him.

As for the Empress, she had, as we have seen, borne herself wonderfully well in the first moments which had followed upon the tragedy, but afterward her nerves gave way entirely, and it was then that she had to be kept in strict seclusion, and under the care of trained nurses. It was said that her reason had given way under the load of her anxiety for her small son, and that the thought of his serious condition had weighed down so thoroughly on her mind that she had grown melancholy to an alarming extent. The story was believed perhaps because it suited so many people to think that it was true, and, besides, the political situation in Russia was becoming so alarming that it entirely absorbed public attention. The war with Japan had come to an ignominious end, and shown the many failings, as well as the thorough insufficiency, of the Government. The first symptoms of the Revolution were clearly appearing on the horizon, with its attendant horrors. Everybody felt that something had to be done in order to avert a catastrophe the extent of which it was impossible to foresee, but which was generally considered as being inevitable, unless the Czar made up his mind to grant the reforms for which his whole Empire was clamoring.

During those years, which were the prelude of other even more eventful ones that were later on to sweep away the Throne of the Romanoffs, Nicholas II. might still have regained the popularity which he had lost. If he had only bravely and courageously faced his people, and tried to get into direct contact with them, he could have secured for his dynasty a new lease of life. He was not liked, it is true, and he was not trusted, which was still worse; but nations are sometimes apt to be led by impulse, and it is certain that Russia would have felt grateful to him if he had only made an appeal to its loyalty for his person, and asked of her to help him in the task of repairing the wounds caused by the disastrous campaign that had come to an end with the signature of the Treaty of Portsmouth.

But the Czar ignored the wishes of his subjects and refused to acknowledge the justice of their claims to be taken into his confidence. He was narrow-minded, cruel by disposition, and though not at all an autocrat, yet every inch a tyrant. He was even something worse than that; he was a coward, and this is a defect which neither nations nor women forgive in those to whom they find their destinies intrusted.

The remembrance of that dreadful Sunday when a crowd of peaceful workmen, under the leadership of the afterward notorious priest, Gapone, marched toward the Winter Palace, to be met with the firing of machine-guns that laid them low by hundreds on the pavement—the remembrance of this bloody deed has never been effaced from the mind of the Russian nation. It traced between itself and its Czar a line of demarcation which could never be removed later on.

Many versions exist as to the conduct of Nicholas II. on that awful day. Some people have said that it was the Empress who had entreated him to fly to Tsarskoye Selo, where she thought that they would be in greater safety than in St. Petersburg; others have asserted that it was he who of his own accord had decided that it would be better for him to leave the capital and to abandon to his uncle, the

Grand-Duke Wladimir, the task of drowning in blood this attempt of his subjects to enter into direct communication with him. Probably both versions are right, in a sense, at least, because it is certain that Alexandra Feodorowna was always in fear something might happen to her son, and very likely she tried to induce her husband to consider how best to insure the safety of their only boy; on the other hand, the Emperor might, had he only come himself to take a sane view of the situation such as it presented itself at the time, have been able to reassure his wife and to explain to her that neither she nor their children were in any danger. Nicholas II., however, had only one thought in his small mind, and that was how to punish this "insolence," as he termed it, of his people. For him a mob was always a mob, except when it was ordered to cheer him, and lately he had had to acknowledge that, in regard to St. Petersburg, cheering had become rather a rare event.

I am not trying to relate here any of the numerous episodes which have made the unsuccessful Revolution of 1905 memorable. I am not writing the history of Nicholas II. Others have done so, and will do so, better than I could. What I only want to point out is the utter callousness shown by both the Czar and the Czarina in presence of the abominable repression which the police, together with some military commanders, inaugurated in regard to the people compromised even in a slight degree in the movement of emancipation which had shaken the existence of the dynasty. It was in vain that some wise people, like Count Witte, for instance, had tried to explain to Nicholas II. that unless he frankly granted some reforms without which it would be impossible to govern Russia in the future he might expect an explosion of wrath on the part of the nation which it would be almost impossible to subdue or to destroy. The Czar refused to listen, and when at last he yielded to the demands of his Ministry and signed the famous Manifest of the 17th of October, with its "simulacre" of constitution, it was with the firm intention not to keep any of the promises which it contained, and to try, on the contrary, to reduce to absolute powerlessness the National Assembly, or Duma, as it was called, the election of which he had allowed only because he could not help it, but not at all because he believed or hoped it might prove useful to him in the solution of the many problems which were waiting to be unraveled.

What followed upon the first convocation of the first Parliament Russia was to know is already a matter of history. It did not live for more than a few weeks, and very probably the Czar had never intended it to exist for any length of time. What he wished was to appear before the eyes of Europe as a Sovereign who had been willing to make any amount of sacrifices in order to insure the welfare of his subjects, who, instead of showing themselves grateful to him for his good intentions, had rewarded him with the basest ingratitude. He thought this a clever piece of policy, forgetting that any politician worthy of the name could see at once through his game, and that this game could have only one result—that of inspiring an utter contempt for his person as well as for his moral character.

Therein lies the great, the supreme, fault of Nicholas II. He never could bring himself to act frankly in regard to any serious matter in which his people were concerned. The Empress, in her strange way, was far more honest, because she did not hesitate to follow the instincts of her heart, and in her most mistaken actions she was at least sincere.

During the years that followed upon the insurrectionary movement of 1905 Alexandra Feodorowna was in such a state of health that it was almost impossible for her to take any part in what went on around her. Her reason had been seriously compromised by the shock caused by the tragical ending of the only romance she had known in her life, and she used to spend hours weeping in her room, absorbed in the contemplation of her own grief. It was in vain that Anna Wyrubewa, who had become more intimate with her than had even been the case before, had tried to induce her to fight the morbid ideas which were torturing her. The Empress would not listen to her friend, and insisted on secluding herself from the world and even from her own daughters, whose presence irritated her and made her give way to fits of impatience that were very nearly akin to madness. The girls were perfectly charming and had the luck to have an excellent governess, who tried to give them the love their own mother refused or was unable to award them; nevertheless their lives were blighted by the illness of the Empress, and it is not extraordinary that they came to care for their father more than for her, whom they were always more or less afraid to approach, whom they were constantly told they must not bother by questions of any kind or manifestations of affection.

It was only the little Cesarewitsch who was allowed to share his mother's solitude, whom she would never let out of her sight. He was the only preoccupation her diseased mind would admit, and when she saw that his state of health did not improve she became more and more desperate, until one day she confided to Anna Wyrubewa that she was sure God was punishing her for the affection which she acknowledged now that she had borne for Orloff, and that her boy would never get well. Her despair was so evident, and her mind was getting so unhinged, that at last the question of putting her in some retreat where she could be under a doctor's continual care was seriously considered by her medical attendants, who even informed the Czar of their fears in regard to the sanity of his Consort. Of course the fact that they had done so reached the knowledge of Madame Wyrubewa, and it was then that the latter began to consider whether it would not be possible to restore by some way or other the equanimity of Alexandra Feodorowna and to procure for her some kind of consolation for the seemingly incurable grief which was destroying her life and her reason. Unfortunately for all parties concerned, she was to make at that time the acquaintance of the notorious Raspoutine, whom she introduced, under the circumstances which I am going presently to relate, to the miserable, half-demented Empress, an introduction which was to prove so fatal not only to the unhappy Sovereign, but also through her to the whole of Russia.

CHAPTER XV

A PROPHET OF GOD

ANNA WYRUBEWA had always been inclined toward religious exaggeration, and this was perhaps one of the reasons why the Empress, who for years had buried herself in the exercise of all kinds of devotional practices, had taken to her so quickly. They were both of a mystical turn of mind, and never so happy as when enabled to spend long hours absorbed in prayer before some icon or other. And besides this, Anna was in the habit of frequenting certain circles of St. Petersburg society that were considered as the supporters of orthodoxy in its most rigid form, where all questions concerning the discipline of the Church were discussed and in some cases decided.

Such, for instance, was the house of the Countess Sophy Ignatieff, where the higher clergy used to meet at weekly assemblies, during which the laxity of the younger generation in regard to religious matters was discussed with many a sigh and many a shaking of wise heads, disposed to admit that this religious indifference, which was getting stronger and stronger every day, was bound to bring Russia to the brink of terrible misfortunes. Countess Ignatieff had traveled all over her native country in search of its sacred shrines and places, and was very well known personally in almost all the principal convents in the Empire. She had been suspected at one time of sympathies with dissenters, but this has never been proved; on the contrary, in her old age she gained the reputation of being fanatically orthodox, one who saw no salvation outside the fold of her own creed, who favored persecution of all others on account of her conviction that people ought to be brought back to the bosom of the Greek Church by any means, even through violence if other ones failed.

During one of the yearly pilgrimages in which so much of her time was spent she had had occasion to meet a kind of vagrant preacher whose wild eloquence had captivated her fancy and her imagination, and she had been partly instrumental in his coming to St. Petersburg, where she had arranged for him to hold religious meetings in her house, to which she had invited prominent church dignitaries, together with a few ladies of an enthusiastic turn of mind whom she believed would be inclined to listen to the wild ravings, for they were nothing else, of her new *protégé*.

At first people laughed at her, as well as at the uncouth appearance of the "Prophet of God," as she called him, who, while not blessed with the eloquence of a Savonarola, yet possessed sufficient persuasive gifts and talents to shake the equanimity of the hysterically inclined women who listened to him. This "Prophet" was none other than Grigory Raspoutine, who later on was to become such an important personage in Russia.

Madame Wyrubewa had heard about Raspoutine a long time before she ever came to hear him. But after she had had the opportunity of meeting him she thought that it would not be a bad thing to bring him to Tsarskoye Selo, where the poor Empress was eating away her heart in her grief at the loss of all that she had cared for in life, and to try to induce Alexandra to listen to him, and to pray together with him. He was supposed to perform wonders by the intensity and the fervor of his prayers, and it might just be possible that the very fact of his being a complete stranger to her, and moreover a man totally outside Court circles and Court intrigues, would influence the Czarina to give him her confidence and to permit him to cheer her up. At all events, she spoke about him several times, and pleaded hard with the Empress to allow him to be brought to her. This Alexandra Feodorowna absolutely refused, but she was induced at last to consent to see him at the house of Anna Wyrubewa, and thither came one winter evening the adventurer who was in time to become the Cagliostro of a reign which was not even worthy to have any one else but a common, uncouth peasant for its jester.

Now, as has been ultimately proved, Raspoutine was far from being the saintly man his admirers thought he was, but he was endowed with an unusual amount of cunning, and far more spirit of observation than he was credited with. When he was told that he would have the honor of meeting the Empress of Russia, and to pray in her presence for the health of her delicate little boy, he had at once perceived the advantages which might result for him out of this introduction, if only in regard to his personal prestige before his disciples and followers. He was above everything else a man who cared for his enjoyment as well as for the good things of life, and who, in the way of Paradise, only admitted the one described by Mohammed in his Koran. He had led a licentious, godless kind of existence, which he had contrived to persuade the weak women who had succumbed to his exhortations was in accord with the spirit of the doctrine which he preached, the principal points of which consisted in blind submission to his will and to his fancies. He had told them that they would be cleansed of their sins by a complete union with him, which he meant in the physical as well as in the moral sense of the word. It is probable that in his dealings with all the people who had grown to believe in him he had had recourse to his incontestable hypnotical powers and to practices of magnetic influence which he had learned amid some wild tribes of Siberia, where he had spent his childhood and early youth, who are to this day adepts in the art of witchcraft as well as in all kinds of magical rites and customs. At the same time the crafty adventurer knew very well that it would be unwise of him at the beginning of his intercourse with the Consort of his Sovereign, an intercourse which he was fully determined should be continued and not be limited to a single interview, to do aught else but assume the attitude of a man entirely absorbed in God and in the practices of religion. When he was introduced to Alexandra Feodorowna at the house of Anna Wyrubewa, he therefore remained standing before her, in an attitude of apparent humility, and he waited quietly until she should begin talking with him, which she immediately did, saying that she had heard so much about him that she had wished to see him and to ask him to pray for her little boy, whose state of health gave rise to so much anxiety and worry.

Raspoutine looked at her, then replied quietly that he would be happy to pray for the child, but that he thought she was just as much in need of prayer as her son because her state of moral health was far more alarming than Alexis's physical one.

The Empress was so amazed that she could not find a reply to what appeared to her in the first moment to be an unsurpassed piece of insolence. Anna Wyrubewa saw what was taking place in her mind, and, addressing her in English, a language which they always spoke together, implored her not to feel offended, as the man really did not know what he was saying, sometimes being urged by a strength superior to his own to give utterance to thoughts he would never have dared to express otherwise. She then urged the Czarina not to carry on the conversation further, but to ask Raspoutine to begin at once praying for her welfare, and also for that of Russia and of the Imperial Family.

Alexandra acquiesced, and the preacher proceeded to set himself before the icon which, as is usual in all Russian houses, was hanging in a corner of the room. He began long litanies which he recited in a peculiar deep tone of voice, that rose up louder and louder as gradually he worked himself up into a state of religious frenzy akin to the one displayed by the dancing and howling dervishes in Turkey. But whether or not his manner or the tone of his supplications or his personal influence was the cause of it, the Empress as she listened to him felt calmer and quieter than she had done for years. It seemed to her as if a great peace was stealing upon her after the despair and the sadness in which her days had been spent during the last months. When at last Raspoutine's orisons came to an end she was weeping silently, but all the nervous excitement under which she had been laboring at the beginning of the interview seemed to have disappeared and she looked more like a normal woman than she had done since the day when Orloff had said his last good-by to her in the boudoir of Anna Wyrubewa.

She silently extended her hand to the "Prophet," saying as she did so:

"You have done me a great deal of good, and I thank you with all my heart. I shall ask you again to pray for me."

It was thus that Alexandra Feodorowna met the man who was to have such a baneful influence over her whole life, whose fatal influence was to estrange her, still deeper than was already the case, from her subjects, and to give rise to the flood of calumnies in which she was ultimately to be drowned; and to perish, dragging along with her this mighty Russian Empire whose Crown she wore and whose people she had never understood nor even tried to understand.

Anna Wyrubewa was delighted to see that her beloved Czarina had really found some comfort in listening to Raspoutine's prayers. She believed in the "Prophet" who had found favor in the eyes of the Lord, and whose intercession in regard to the little Alexis would be crowned with success. The woman was superstitious to the backbone, and perhaps more mystically inclined even than most

Russians are, which is saying a good deal. She thought, at all events, that, once the Empress got to be persuaded that she had to look to God alone for the recovery of her son from a disease that had been pronounced to be incurable by the best medical authorities, she would no longer fret as she had done, but begin to look at things from a religiously fatalistic point of view. She hoped also for another thing, and that was that the Czarina, once she had been taught to look above for comfort and consolation, would cease to lament over the "might have been" that has already caused so much heartburnings in this world, and that she would leave off reproaching herself, as she was constantly doing, for the death of the one man she had cared for, whom in all innocence she had sent to his destruction, and who had bravely preferred to disappear rather than allow a stain to rest upon her honor. She had guessed the agony of the self-reproach under which the soul of Alexandra Feodorowna had almost collapsed, and the remorse which had racked it until her intelligence had almost snapped, through the moral as well as through the physical pain which had clouded all her faculties. She hoped, therefore, seriously and earnestly, that the prayers of Raspoutine might ease this mental distress which had transformed the Empress of All the Russias into a half-demented woman. When she saw that his prayers had over the latter the beneficent influence she had expected, she determined to do her best to induce her to give her confidence to this man in whom her exalted imagination saw a savior as well as a friend.

This was the real beginning of the Raspoutine intrigue, and it would have been a lucky thing for all those who came afterward to be concerned in it if it had stopped at this stage, and not been transferred to a more dangerous one, the stage upon which European politics had to be played and, unfortunately for Russia, played by utterly unskilful hands. The comedy of Raspoutine did not last longer than a few months. Its drama dragged on for years, and is not yet over by a long way.

CHAPTER XVI

SHE SAW HIM ONCE MORE

AFTER she had made the acquaintance of Raspoutine the Empress changed considerably. For one thing, she became more cheerful and seemed once more to interest herself in what went on around her. She tried also to keep her mind away from the one morbid thought which had been haunting her, the thought that her son's bad health was a punishment which God had sent her on account of her conduct in regard to Colonel Orloff. She had most undoubtedly loved the young officer, and she realized with a painful but clear perspicacity that if she had allowed him to go away when he wished to do so the tragedy which had culminated with his suicide would never have taken place. Her mind, which was dimmed as to so many other points, was quite awake to the terrible one that the man to whom her whole heart had belonged had died to save her honor and to prevent her good name from being compromised. This was quite sufficient to fill her soul with acute remorse, but apart from this she missed the companionship of this faithful friend before whom she could allow herself to speak about her sorrows and her trials just as if she had been an ordinary woman and not an Empress.

There were times when her grandeur oppressed her, and then it was that she longed for a confidant and friend before whom she would not be ashamed to bare her heart and unburden it. She felt so lonely amid the pomp and splendor which surrounded her, so solitary in her great Palace which was so very different from the simple house in which her childhood and youth had been spent, and she was such a stranger in a land she had not learned to love and where she had found herself confronted with hostility from the very first day that she had set her foot in it. Of course her children, and especially her son, constituted a great interest and a great preoccupation in her life, but their existence was not sufficient to fill it entirely. In moments when she thought herself forsaken by the world she would have given ten years of her future existence to be able to see once more the man who had died for her because he had found it impossible to consecrate his whole life to her service.

Raspoutine was a keen observer of human nature. Lurking behind his hopeless ignorance there were immense cunning and a natural intuition of what was going on in other people's minds. Apart from this faculty, he always made it a point to try and find out as much as he could concerning the past of all persons with whom he happened to have dealings. He understood quite admirably the art of "drawing out" those with whom he conversed, and he could put together quite nicely the tangled threads which another man would never have gone to the trouble of trying to untwine. As soon as he had looked upon the Empress he had understood that she must have gone through some great grief which was not concerned with the state of health of her child alone, but which had deeper foundations. In the fashionable drawing-rooms where he was a welcome guest he had heard discussed more than once the personality as well as the conduct of Alexandra Feodorowna; he had come to the conclusion that the mystery which surrounded the death of Colonel Orloff was in some way connected with her, and not with Madame Wyrubewa alone. He applied himself, therefore, to discover what had really taken place.

For some time he could learn nothing, as no one seemed to know anything more than the bare fact of the suicide of the young officer. It is true that when he had asked Anna for the true version the latter had angrily denied any connection implying guilt, but Raspoutine, peasant though he was, understood sufficiently the character of a woman of the world to know that such denials were not worth much. Altogether he was puzzled, but continued, however, to put in an appearance at Tsarskoye Selo whenever he was asked to do so, and he was shown several times the little Heir to the Throne. The Empress had brought the babe to Madame Wyrubewa's cottage several times for him to pray over. The "Prophet" had at once declared that the child would not die, and that there was every likelihood he would outgrow his weakness, a prophecy it had been relatively easy for him to make, considering the fact that before doing so he had taken good care to talk with a doctor of his acquaintance about the illness of Alexis, and had heard from him all that there was to hear on the subject, which was not much. The boy might live with care, and even get strong, once he had reached the years of adolescence; he might die from the effect of a hemorrhage, which the slightest accident might bring about. The whole thing was a matter of chance, and nothing else.

The Empress, however, became full of hope when Raspoutine told her not to worry unnecessarily, but to trust more to Providence than she had been doing. It happened just at that time that the little boy got stronger and better than he had been since his birth, and this fact inspired her with a hope such as she had never allowed herself to nurse since the day when she had realized to what a weak and frail piece of humanity she had given birth in the person of the only son and Heir of Nicholas II. She began to speak of the future, which she had hitherto not dared to do, and she seemed suddenly to think that this future might still hold some joys for her in reserve. As was but natural, she attributed this change in her feelings and mind to the influence of Raspoutine's prayers, and as was also natural she felt grateful to him for having brought it about.

The crafty peasant, however, was not so satisfied as the Empress. He had begun to make great plans concerning her and the influence he meant to acquire over her person. Somehow he could not bring them to realization. He might have gone on for a long time in this state of uncertainty if he had not made just at that moment the acquaintance of one of the cleverest secret police agents the Russian Government had in its pay, Manassavitch-Maniuloff. This personage, whom I have described at length in another book, knew more about what went on in the Imperial Palace of Tsarskoye Selo than any one else in the world. During the time when the famous Plehwe occupied the post of Minister of the Interior he had had the Palace watched just as much as the houses of the people whom he suspected of not favoring his views and policy. Among the agents whom he had intrusted with this task Manassavitch-Maniuloff had occupied a foremost place. He was one of the most unscrupulous men alive, and, as the future proved, had but one aim in his existence, that of enriching himself, thanks to all kinds of shady speculations and blackmail he practised on a large scale. He knew, if others did not, all that had taken place in the house of Anna Wyrubewa on the day when Colonel Orloff had left it for the last time, but he had never divulged this secret, and had been content with waiting patiently until the day when he might be able to turn it into account and to make capital out of it. Always on the alert, and just as keen an observer as Raspoutine himself of the weaknesses of human nature, with the additional advantage of being a very well educated and cultured man, he very quickly grasped the importance of what the "Prophet" confided to him when he started to relate to his friend the details of his first interview with the Empress of All the Russias.

Maniuloff was very well posted as to all the details of the Philippe incident, together with its ridiculous end. When he had heard how much Alexandra Feodorowna had been impressed by the fervor of Raspoutine's prayers, he suggested to the latter that he make use of the hypnotic faculties which he possessed in order to get the inexperienced and weak-minded Sovereign to become a tool in the hands of both. He gave him very detailed instructions as to how he was to proceed.

Armed with these instructions, Raspoutine started upon a campaign which brought Mr. Maniuloff to penal servitude, sent the Czarina to exile in Siberia, and himself to an untimely and bloody grave.

At the meetings at Anna Wyrubewa's house, during which the "Prophet" not only prayed himself for the prosperity of the House of Romanoff, he also persuaded the Empress to pray, too, in accordance with the particular rites which he declared were indispensable to a perfect communion of the human spirit with God, and which consisted in numerous genuflexions, and other things of the same kind; in long fasts and hours spent in meditation with the face on the floor, in what grew in time to be a hysterical state of ecstasy. These meetings went on undisturbed for a considerable length of time, until one day Raspoutine informed Alexandra Feodorowna that he thought it wiser to discontinue them because certain things had been revealed to him by the Holy Ghost which had caused him to think that it would be better if he went away; otherwise he would be compelled to try and take her spiritually with him into regions whither perhaps she would not care to follow him. The Empress, of course, eagerly asked what he meant, upon which he replied that to perfect people such as he and she the Lord could grant the privilege of entering into relations with dead and gone people whom they had loved in this world; he did not know whether she would be able to go through this ordeal; therefore he thought it better to discontinue their meetings for the present.

The Czarina went home brooding upon what she had heard and with all her superstitious curiosity awakened. At first she tried not to think of what the "Prophet" had told her. Then she wondered whether she would be strong enough to face the ordeal of entering into communion with the other world, that world for which she had been longing, where had gone the one man she had loved beyond every other earthly thing. For some weeks she struggled against the temptation as it had been presented to her by Raspoutine; then at last she yielded to it, and asked Anna Wyrubewa to bring the "Prophet" once more to her house, as she wanted to speak with him again.

The adventurer demurred at first, finding one obstacle after another in order to decline the invitation which had been extended to him. At last he consented to an interview, but declared that he would insist that no one else be present at it, as the things which the "spirit" had commanded him to say to Alexandra Feodorowna were of such a secret nature that no one but herself could hear them. When he was introduced into the presence of the Sovereign he began by falling on his knees and praying with a fervor such as she had never seen him display before. At last he told the miserable, deluded woman that he had been commanded to say to her that there was one pure spirit now in another world who had been allowed to communicate with her through his medium; that he did not know who it was, but that if she wished to try the experiment she must, before attempting it, prepare herself for it, with long prayers and fastings, so as to be in a complete state of grace; otherwise the favor about to be conferred on her could not be awarded. By that time the Czarina had reached a nervous condition where anything Raspoutine told her would have been acceptable to her over-excited brain. She promised to conform herself to all the directions given to her, and three days later she met again the impostor in a place which he indicated to her, whither she went, accompanied by the faithful Anna. Madame Wyrubewa, however, was not admitted to the room where Raspoutine was waiting for the Empress. He stood before several holy images, with lamps burning before them.

The Empress had scarcely touched any food for three days; she had spent the time in long and almost continual orisons. She was just in a condition when any appeal to her superstition would be sure to meet with response. When she prostrated herself beside the "Prophet," she had reached a state of exhaustion and excitement which made her an easy prey to any imposture practised by the unscrupulous. For about an hour Raspoutine kept praying aloud, invoking the spirits of heaven in an impressive voice, every word of which went deep into the heart of Alexandra Feodorowna. Suddenly he seized her by the arm, exclaiming as he did so: "Look! look! and then believe!"

She raised her eyes, and saw distinctly on the white wall the image of Colonel Orloff, which, by a clever trick had been flashed on it by a magic lantern held for the purpose by Manassavitch-Maniuloff.

The Empress gave one terrible cry and fell in a dead faint on the floor. Anna Wyrubewa, hearing her scream of agony, rushed into the room to find nothing but Raspoutine absorbed in deep prayer beside the inanimate form of his victim.

This was but the first scene of many of the same character. The Czarina recovered her scared senses with the full conviction that she had really seen the spirit of the man she had loved so dearly; she was very soon persuaded that he had been allowed to show himself to her and that he would henceforward watch over her and guide her with advice and encouragement in her future life. She quite believed that Raspoutine, whom she sincerely thought to be in total ignorance as to that episode in her life, was a real Prophet of God, and that, thanks to him, she would be able to communicate with the dead. Whether Anna Wyrubewa shared this conviction or not it is difficult to say, but it is not likely that either Raspoutine or Maniuloff confided in her. They knew too well the small reliance that, as a rule, can be placed upon feminine secrecy, and the game they were playing was far too serious for them to run the risk of compromising it by an indiscretion. It is therefore far more probable that they also played upon the superstitious feelings of the Empress's friend, and that they used both ladies for the furtherance of their own nefarious schemes with as much unscrupulousness as consummate art.

CHAPTER XVII

MY SON! I MUST SAVE MY SON!

AFTER the episode which I have just related, there was no longer any question of Raspoutine being allowed to leave the proximity of the Imperial Court. The Empress came to have such utter confidence in him that she even tried to induce the Czar to consult him; this he refused to do, but, seeing how much brighter his wife had become since her acquaintance with the "Prophet," he made no objection to her seeing him.

One must here remark that both Raspoutine and his chief adviser, Manassavitch-Maniuloff, played their cards wonderfully well by avoiding every appearance of mixing themselves up with politics. The "Prophet" talked with the Empress when he had the opportunity to do so, which, by the way, was not so frequent as might have been supposed. His conversations were always confined to religious subjects. He was very carefully coached by his accomplice every time he had to meet Alexandra Feodorowna, and he used to relate to her some sensational supernatural stories, which a man of his ignorance could not possibly have learned if he had not been inspired by the Almighty, as she fondly imagined. Her superstitious feelings had entirely taken the upper hand of her reason in all matters where Raspoutine was concerned, and she truly believed him to be a Prophet of God, whose every word was inspired by Heaven, whose intercession in her behalf had decided the Almighty to cure her son of a disease which all the doctors who had seen him had pronounced to be quite incurable.

In the mean while, although the relations of the Czarina with the crafty adventurer who had succeeded in captivating her confidence remained restricted to the purely religious ground, people were talking about them, trying to turn them into a vast agency where everything in the world could be bought and sold, providing the necessary money was forthcoming to do it. Manassavitch-Maniuloff, thanks to the numerous spies whose services he could command for a consideration, started to spread the rumor that Raspoutine had become all powerful in Court circles, and that if only one applied to him one could bring through the most difficult kind of business. It must be remembered that at the time I am referring to (the five years or so immediately preceding the war) Russia had been transformed into a vast stock-exchange, thanks to the mania for speculation which, since the Japanese war, had seized hold of the public. Industry always more or less neglected had suddenly taken a new and unexpected lease of life, and banks did a roaring business in selling and buying for the account of the innumerable speculators who rushed to invest their money. Nothing mattered in that respect save the quotation of yesterday and the one expected or hoped for to-morrow.

Government contracts for all kinds of things, especially contracts connected with the railway business and with factories of every sort, were eagerly sought for. In the fight which was taking place to obtain them every possible argument was employed. The art of Maniuloff and of his friends, because he was not alone in this detestable business, consisted in persuading others, even men in power who ought to have known better, that Raspoutine, through his connection with the powers who ruled at Tsarskoye Selo, could get for them such contracts that he expected in return a solid commission, which, of course, was never refused to him.

How long this kind of thing would have gone on it is difficult to say if Mr. Stolypine, who was at the time Prime Minister, had not had his attention drawn toward the activity of the "Prophet." Not knowing very well what to make of the conflicting reports which were brought to him, he expressed one day the desire to meet Raspoutine. After the interview he uttered his famous phrase:

"The only use the man could be put to was to light the furnace of the house he was living in."

The words were repeated, of course, to the person whom they concerned, and they proved the death sentence of Stolypine, because his "removal" by fair or by foul means was decided immediately after he had uttered them. Stolypine, however, in spite of his apparent disdain for the strange personality of Raspoutine, was far too clever not to realize that the constant presence of this man by the side of the Empress of Russia was likely to lead to gossip of a dangerous kind, if not to various complications. He tried at first to get rid of him by diplomatic means, and enrolled the sympathies of the Grand-Duchess Elisabeth, the eldest sister of Alexandra Feodorowna, who, by reason of her having embraced a religious life, was in possession of great respect everywhere and could say what she liked to the Czar as well as to the Czarina. The Prime Minister explained to her that it was to the highest degree harmful for the reputation of the Imperial dynasty in general to see its heads give way to a superstition which only evoked ridicule on the part of reasonable people. Elisabeth Feodorowna promised that she would try what she could do, but after a while she had to acknowledge that at the first words she had spoken concerning the advisability of sending Raspoutine back to his native village of Pokrowskoye in Siberia the Empress had interrupted her so angrily that she had not been able to go on with the conversation.

Stolypine was not a man to stop at half-measures. He asked no one's law or leave, and in virtue of his powers as Prime Minister he had the "Prophet" exiled from the capital at twenty-four hours' notice.

Raspoutine wished to communicate with the Empress as soon as the order to leave St. Petersburg was signified to him, but he was prevented from doing so by his friend, Manassavitch-Maniuloff, who assured him that it would be far wiser not to murmur, and to accept the decree of banishment issued against him; because in that way he would acquire far more sympathy than would be the case if he rebelled; besides, in his absence it would be relatively easy to play upon the nervous temperament of the Empress to such an extent that after he had been recalled he would never stand again the risk of a second dismissal. This was accordingly done and Alexandra Feodorowna found herself alone, deprived of the possibility of going on with religious practices that had gradually assumed the character of those indulged in by that sect of the Khlystys to which Raspoutine belonged.

By a strange coincidence, which was nothing but a coincidence because, weak and foolish as was Anna Wyrubewa, she did not lend herself to the conspiracy which was so falsely attributed to her, which in reality did not exist, the conspiracy of drugging the little Cesarewitsch for the purpose of proving to his mother that he could not be well so long as Raspoutine was not there to pray for him—the child suddenly sickened in a more dangerous manner than ever before. The poor Empress again went out of her mind. She used to cry aloud that God was punishing her for not having known how to protect His "Prophet," and things of the same kind. At last the baby grew better, and the Court could remove to the Crimea, where it was hoped he would more rapidly recover than in the damp climate of St. Petersburg. It was during this journey that Stolypine was murdered by secret police agents, a crime in which it was generally believed that Raspoutine, together with his accomplices, had been mixed up. The Empress, who had hated the Prime Minister ever since she had ascertained that it was he who had banished her favorite, did not disarm even in the presence of death, and it was related that she publicly prided herself upon having persuaded the Emperor not to attend the funeral of the man who had died for him, but to leave Kieff for Livadia on the eve of the day when it was to take place.

She had become very bitter just then, and she never missed any opportunity which presented itself to show her want of affection for the Imperial Family, as well as her contempt for the Russian people. The morganatic marriage of the only brother of Nicholas II., the Grand-Duke Michael, which took place at about that time, procured her a new occasion to prove the unbounded influence which since the birth of her son she had acquired over the mind of the weak Emperor, and to exercise her revengeful feelings in an unexpected manner. This marriage, so much must be conceded, was of a nature to give rise to unpleasantness, and could not in any case have been viewed with favorable eyes either by the Czar or by the Imperial Family. The lady had already been divorced twice, and the fact of her last husband having been an officer in the same regiment as the Grand Duke was also a reason why the match would have been disapproved of in any case. But, on the other hand, Michael Alexandrowitch, in uniting himself to the woman who had captivated his heart and his fancy, was acting as a man of honor, considering several facts which made it almost imperative for him not to forsake a person who had sacrificed much for his sake. It would certainly have been sufficient to oblige him to leave the army and to reside for some time abroad as a punishment, and no one imagined that worse could befall him.

The Empress had always intensely disliked her brother-in-law, who would have been Regent of the Empire in case the Czar had died before the Heir to the Throne had reached his majority, and she determined to make use of the opportunity which had arisen to vent her bad feelings on a man in whom she saw a rival to the claims of her own son. She induced Nicholas II. to deprive the Grand Duke of his fortune as well as of his civil rights, and to make out of him a ward in chancery. The scandal was immense, and it did not procure any friends for Alexandra Feodorowna.

In the mean while the Cesarewitsch sickened again, and the frantic mother implored Anna Wyrubewa to write to Raspoutine and to implore the latter to work a miracle of some kind in favor of her son. The "Prophet" replied that he would pray with all his heart for the child, but that he doubted very much whether this would avail, because the Empress had neglected her duties in regard to the Almighty and forgotten to continue the practices of mortification and of devotion she had been wrapped up in the whole time he had been near her to urge her to go on with them. Alexandra Feodorowna could not stand this last reproach, and she forthwith started to implore the Czar to recall the "Prophet." But Nicholas II. had been warned against him quite recently and refused to grant her request. This brought about a renewal of tears and hysterics on the part of the Czarina, and at last, one day that she was alone with Anna, she unburdened her soul to the latter, exclaiming that she knew her beloved boy was going to die and that it would be her fault, ending her confession with the agonized cry:

"My son! I must save my son!"

Madame Wyrubewa saw that the poor creature was in such an over-excited state that she might really be facing a collapse of her reason. She then proposed to the infatuated Alexandra to have recourse to a bold measure, which consisted in bringing back Raspoutine quite secretly to St. Petersburg, where he could stay at her house without any one getting to hear of it. If, then, his prayers brought about the amelioration required in the state of health of the little Alexis, the Empress would be able to tell the Czar what she had done, and perhaps to convince the latter of the efficacy of the holy man's intervention and intercession on behalf of their boy.

The Czarina caught eagerly at the idea, and after long negotiations, which very nearly failed because Raspoutine did not yield at once to the entreaties sent to him, he at last consented to return to St. Petersburg. He was secretly introduced into the room where the Heir to the Russian Throne was lying, in what every one thought were already the throes of death. He prayed for the child, he prayed for the Empress, and he urged the latter to submit to certain mysterious passes which he proceeded to perform over her head. A few days after this secret interview Alexis suddenly began to improve; not only this, but he became stronger and brighter than he had been for a long time.

Alexandra Feodorowna was radiant, and one day when Nicholas II. was rejoicing at the happy change which had taken place in the condition of their son she informed him of what she had done and begged from him permission to bring Raspoutine to him and to allow him to remain in the vicinity of the Court in the future. Nicholas II. was convinced and granted the necessary authorization. After this the question of Raspoutine's return to Siberia was not raised again, and he never left, except for short vacations, the Sovereigns who had at last been persuaded to give to him their complete confidence.

The Palace of Tsarskoye Selo

He refused, however, to take up his abode in Tsarskoye Selo, and showed himself very discreet in his demeanor. He was admirably advised, and he prepared himself in silence for the part it was intended for him to play in the future. But at stated intervals, and upon stated days, he used to see the Empress, either in her own rooms or, most frequently, at the house of Anna Wyrubewa, when he evoked for her the spirit of Colonel Orloff and transmitted messages which he was supposed to have received. Alexandra Feodorowna believed him, and this new understanding, which she firmly thought had, thanks to the prayers of the "Prophet," established itself between her and the man who had possessed her heart, proved to her the greatest consolation she had known. It induced her to come out of her retirement and to begin to take part in the management of public affairs, which she insisted upon the Czar communicating to her. The time was coming when it would become known in Russia that if the Sovereign was a weak man his Consort was trying to show herself a strong woman, and comparisons between Alexandra Feodorowna and Catherine the Great began to be heard in the yet small circle which affected to admire the new qualities it prided itself upon having discovered in the young Empress.

CHAPTER XVIII

ANOTHER WAR

THE years which followed upon Raspoutine's triumphant return to Tsarskoye Selo were most eventful ones for Russia as well as for the Imperial Family. Europe, too, went through political convulsions which were the preliminary of the disaster that was to sweep over it in 1914, but in which very few people in 1912 were able to discern danger. I am referring to the annexation by Austria of Bosnia and Herzegovina and to the two Balkan wars. When Servia was threatened by Bulgarian ambition there existed a powerful party in Russia which would have liked the Czar to interfere on her behalf, and to lend her his aid against King Ferdinand, on one side, and the Austrian spirit of conquest, on the other. Popular feeling was very much in favor of a Russian demonstration, and for some weeks St. Petersburg was the scene of a violent agitation which, in the opinion of many people, was destined to end in a war with the Austro-Hungarian monarchy. It was not a secret that the Servian Government would not have objected, had such a contingency presented itself, and during the whole of the summer and autumn of 1913 different Servian politicians came to Russia to discuss the situation. In Moscow, as well as in St. Petersburg, they applied themselves to the task of awakening in favor of their country the sympathies of all the Russian Slavophils. At one time it seemed as if they were going to succeed and as if the Czar would be compelled to yield to the general wishes of his subjects.

Here Raspoutine interfered, and, thanks to his influence over the Empress, he contrived to prevent the spread of a conflagration which threatened to extend itself far beyond the Balkan Peninsula. It must not be assumed, however, that in doing so he was actuated by any patriotic motives. He was a man for whom the word "patriotism" had absolutely no meaning. But his friends, as well as himself, were plunged head foremost in financial schemes which a war would in all probability have wrecked, and therefore he applied himself with all his energy to set hindrances in the path of the chauvinists who tried to induce the Emperor to assert the might of his Empire, to rush to the rescue of those Slav nationalities that had refused to conform themselves to the anti-Russian policy which Bulgaria had been pursuing ever since King Ferdinand had been put in control of her destinies.

This interference on the part of the "Prophet" in matters which did not concern him in the least became known very quickly, not only in Russia, but also abroad, and one of the most active members of the German Embassy in St. Petersburg, who was *persona grata* in the Wilhelmstrasse, wrote a whole report on the subject, raising at the same time the question as to whether it would not be worth while to try, with the help of substantial arguments, to win Raspoutine over to the idea of a *rapprochement* between Russia and Germany. The latter was steadily making preparations for the war which she was quite determined to provoke within a very few months. She had always worked toward the destruction of the Franco-Russian understanding, which stood in her way, which she feared might come to endanger her dreams of a world-wide Empire. Every effort had been made on the part of the Berlin Court to win over the Czar to the idea of renewing the intimate bonds which, during the whole time of his grandfather's reign, had united the Hohenzollerns and the Romanoffs. When Nicholas II. had repaired to Berlin for the marriage of the Kaiser's only daughter with the son of the Duke of Cumberland he had been made the object of one of the warmest welcomes he had ever received in his life, a welcome which had touched him so much that he had come back to Tsarskoye Selo full of enthusiasm for his Prussian relatives. If the truth need be told, he was also slightly disillusioned as to the advantages which his country might obtain through its alliance with the French Republic. This feeling of distrust which had thus been sown in his mind in regard to the good intentions of his Latin ally was of course at once reported to the Kaiser by the many friends which the latter had in St. Petersburg, and it made him doubly anxious to win over to his side the good-will as well as the sympathies of Nicholas II. At the same time William was very well aware that it was most difficult to rely on anything promised by a man with such a weak character, or rather with such a lack of character, as his Russian cousin. An ally who would continually whisper in the latter's ear all the advantages which a friendly treaty and understanding with Germany could bring to him, as well as to the whole Russian Empire, was indispensable; of course, when it was suggested to those who controlled the actions and the politics of the Wilhelmstrasse that he might be found in the person of the Empress Alexandra's favorite, the Kaiser came very quickly to the conclusion it would be worth while to obtain the good offices of this remarkable man.

This, however, would have proved difficult, even for the experienced spies which Prussia maintained in all circles of Russian society, as it was not easy to discover means of getting into contact with the formidable adventurer whose name had already become one of the most powerful to conjure with in the vast Russian Empire. At this juncture Mr. Manassavitch-Maniuloff interfered and volunteered his services to William II. The crafty fox had heard that the Czar's confidence in France was slightly shaken. Maniuloff at once bethought himself of the possibility of turning his knowledge to his personal advantage, and he managed, no one knows how, to impart to the German Ambassador in St. Petersburg, Count Pourtalès, his willingness to persuade Nicholas II., through Raspoutine, that he would do well to throw France overboard and to conclude a treaty with the Prussian Government, which eventually might prove of immense advantage to himself by assuring him of German protection in the not improbable case of a new Revolution taking place in his Empire.

This sort of thing went on for some time, and it is quite likely that if events had not precipitated themselves one upon the other with the most startling rapidity, the policy of Raspoutine and his friend might have borne fruit in some way or other, and the relations between the Cabinet of St. Petersburg and that of Paris, which had already sensibly cooled down, would have become even fresher than was already the case. In fact, the announced visit of President Poincaré had not appealed to the Czar, who, while unable to decline it, yet had expressed himself quite loudly as to the small amount of pleasure which he expected to get out of it. Of course Berlin heard about the remarks that had escaped the lips of the Russian Sovereign, and it was not slow to draw its own conclusions from them. In fact, if we are to believe all that was related at the time by persons well up as to what went on in European politics, it was confidently expected by the Kaiser that instead of drawing France and Russia closer together the journey of the French President, thanks to personal frictions he felt sure would arise, would, on the contrary, irritate Nicholas II. and make him look with more favorable eyes than he had done before on the possibility of a change in the conduct of Russian Foreign Affairs.

Whether this would have taken place or not it is difficult to say, because at the last moment Germany lost her most devoted ally, and the influence of the man who had, more than any one else, worked in its interests was eliminated for the time being. A woman, who had just reasons for feeling revengeful against Raspoutine, stabbed him as he was coming out of church in his native village of Pokrowskoye in Siberia, whither he had gone on a short visit. He was ill for a long time, and during the weeks that he was laid up, to the intense consternation of the Empress, who was only with great difficulty prevented from going herself to nurse him, the Austrian ultimatum consequent on the assassination of the Heir to Francis Joseph's Throne was presented to Servia, and followed by the declaration of war launched by Germany almost simultaneously against Russia and France.

This proved for Alexandra Feodorowna the most terrible blow that had yet befallen her since the day when she had plighted her troth to the mighty Czar of All the Russias. During the eventful hours that preceded the initial act of the tragedy which was to change the face of the whole world she went about like a demented woman, crying and praying in turns, and imploring her husband to pause before he allowed the accomplishment of a calamity which she vaguely guessed would claim her for one of its first victims. But this time there was no Raspoutine at her side to play on the feelings of humanity of the weak-minded Nicholas, to persuade him that he ought rather to submit to the humiliation of Russian prestige than to allow another war to throw its shadow on his already too unfortunate reign. On the contrary, all the advisers of the Emperor, all his Ministers, public opinion, the press, and the army, eager to wipe out the remembrance of the Japanese disaster, poured into his ears their conviction that if he did not rush to the help of poor threatened Servia he would not only lose the last fragments of popularity which were left to him, but also put Russia before the whole world in a most shameful and dishonorable position.

As usual, the Czar yielded, with the results which we know and have seen. He could hardly have done anything else, if we take into consideration that Germany was absolutely determined to start the abominable war, from which she hoped to obtain the realization of her schemes of domination of the whole earth. But—and this must be told here—the Kaiser in letters far more authentic than the famous

Willy and Nicky correspondence, which personally I consider as subject to much doubt, in view of certain improbabilities which it contains, the Kaiser did propose at that time to his cousin to conclude with him a defensive and offensive alliance against France and England. In return for which he engaged himself to uphold any designs which Russia might nurse in regard to the Balkans and the Straits.

It may not be to the advantage of his intellectual faculties that Nicholas failed to see the vast political scheme which lay behind this offer; it is certainly to the honor of his moral character that he refused it, and this in spite of the supplications of his wife, who entreated him not to plunge their country into a war which, as she repeated, could only prove disastrous for its future, as well as for that of the dynasty. In spite of his natural defects, of his cruelty, harshness of heart, and utter disregard of the rights of others, the Czar was still a gentleman and he could not be induced to do anything capable of dishonoring him as a gentleman, though he may have lent himself to actions degrading for a Sovereign. During the terribly responsible days which preceded the declaration of war he behaved quite irreproachably. It was later on that he was influenced by Raspoutine and by the Empress to lend himself to political schemes unworthy of him, as well as of the nation over which he ruled.

On the 1st of August, 1914, twelve hours after Germany had thrown her gauntlet into his face, he showed himself for the last time to his people on the balcony of the Winter Palace. An immense crowd had gathered together in the big square which it faces, and for the last time, too, cheered him vociferously, forgetting in this solemn moment all the follies, mistakes, and errors which had saddened his reign and raised a barrier between him and this great Russia that his father had made so prosperous and so mighty. If in that supreme moment he had been able to find words capable of electrifying this crowd into believing in him again, who knows but that the reverses which were to crowd upon him could not have been avoided, or at least diminished! But Nicholas II. never knew how to speak to his subjects or how to touch their hearts. He remained impassible and indifferent in the most critical hours of his life and of theirs, and this incapacity to rise to the height of the situation of the moment was perhaps one of the things which contributed the most to his fall.

I remember him so well on that August afternoon, facing the multitude assembled to greet him as its Czar and leader, and I remember, too, the thought which swept through my mind, that it was a thousand pities it was not his father who stood there in his place. Alexander III. would have known how to address Russia in an hour of national danger. He was neither a brilliant nor an extremely intelligent man, but he was a man and a Sovereign, who realized the duties of a Monarch and of a man. He was, moreover, a Russian who thought and who felt as a Russian alone could think and feel, in questions where the honor and the future of the country were involved. Nicholas II. was simply an Emperor who wished to be an autocrat. It was too much and not enough at the same time, and many among those who looked upon him, as he appeared before his people on that historical balcony whence it was the custom to announce to the population of the capital the death of a Sovereign whenever it took place, many wondered whether they were not going to hear that another one had started on the long journey whence there is no return. His presence seemed to herald a funeral rather than the hope of a triumph, and this impression which he produced was so vivid that more than one acknowledged having experienced it when talking about this famous day which, though we knew it not, proved to be the last upon which a Russian Czar faced the Russian people before the latter overthrew the chief of the House of Romanoff from the Throne which he had disgraced.

CHAPTER XIX

MY FATHERLAND, MUST I FORSAKE THEE?

IT would not have been human on the part of the Empress Alexandra if she had not felt deeply aggrieved at the war which had so unexpectedly broken out between the country of her birth and that of her adoption. She had never really become a Russian at heart and her sympathies had remained exclusively German all through her married life. Apart from this, she had experienced from the intercourse which she had kept up with her own family the only pleasure which she had frankly enjoyed since the Crown of the Russian Czarinas had been put upon her head. She dearly loved her two sisters, the Princess Victoria of Battenberg and the Princess Irene of Prussia, far more, indeed, than she did her other one, the Grand-Duchess Elisabeth, whom she considered more or less as a rival and whom in the secret of her heart she could not forgive for having won in Russia a popularity which had always been denied to her own self.

Then there was her brother, the Grand Duke of Hesse, with whom she had remained in correspondence, who paid her frequent visits in Tsarskoye Selo; there was also her cousin, the Kaiser, who had been the first person to point out to her the responsibilities which were inseparable from the exalted position she occupied as Empress of All the Russias, who had applied himself to persuade her that she had great political talents, and that she could undoubtedly, if she only wished it, become a most important factor in European politics. Strange to say, though she had been brought up partly in England, though her mother had been an English Princess, though she was the grandchild of Queen Victoria, she intensely disliked everything that was English, and had for English customs, English ambitions, and English politics the same hatred which characterized William II. Perhaps this common aversion was one of the reasons why they had always got on so well together, and why they had been able to be of so much use to each other. At all events, the fact that it existed in an equal degree in both of them had drawn them together, and at last, after she had contrived to eliminate the influence of her anti-German mother-in-law, Alexandra Feodorowna had been able to give herself up body and soul to the task of drawing together her husband and her own kindred. She had tried to persuade the former that the only means to insure the prosperity and the welfare of the Russian Empire in the future consisted in a closer union with Germany, with whom there existed absolutely no reason to quarrel, because there were no interests capable of clashing between the two people. She had represented to the weak-minded Nicholas that Russia had obtained from France all that she could hope to get, and that the latter had become weary of always being called upon to invest money in Russian bonds without any return being made for her generosity.

Nicholas II. had always detested republics, and though he had been made much of during his visits to Paris, which he had thoroughly enjoyed, he yet had never felt quite at home amid the Republican society he had been called upon to get acquainted with; in the secret of his heart he despised all French political men, whom he considered as much inferior to himself. But a natural inclination to dissimulation, which he carried so far that many people called it by quite another name, had made him carefully conceal the real state of his feelings in regard to his French ally. It is, however, quite certain that if the war had not broken out the Franco-Russian alliance would have died a natural death. As things occurred, it was for a short space of time to appear more complete than ever; this was not the merit of Nicholas, but the result of the honesty which the French Government brought to bear in all that happened in 1914. In Russian Court circles, which were all of them, more or less, given up to Germany, the news that the country was going to war was received with consternation, and there were many people who declared that it was a shame for Russia to be drawn into a struggle which was essentially a personal quarrel between France and Germany, with which she had nothing to do.

At first and before the anti-German feeling became fierce in St. Petersburg, the Empress, in spite of political complications, remained in private correspondence with her brother, and through him with the Kaiser, to whom she promised that she would spare no efforts to induce the Czar to conclude peace as soon as it became practicable. She had never been able to form an idea of the power which public opinion, especially in times of national danger, can exercise over a nation. She imagined that the authority wielded by the Crown would be sufficient to put an end to any manifestations of sympathy in regard to France on the part of the Russian people. She therefore felt confident that the struggle which had just begun would not last long, and that Russia could come out of it, if not with flying colors, at least without any serious losses.

No one during those early days of the war admitted for one moment the possibility that Warsaw and the line of fortresses which defended the Russian frontier on the side of the Niemen could fall into the hands of the enemy; all that the Empress expected was a defeat of the Russian armies which would not seriously compromise their prestige, but at the same time convince the country that an advantageous peace was, after all, the best way of getting out of a situation where all the time one adversary had either willingly or unwillingly misunderstood the good intentions of the other.

She was consequently working along this line when Raspoutine returned to Tsarskoye Selo. He did this as soon as the doctors had pronounced him fit to travel. She began once more to pray with him and to ask him to put her again into communication with that other world where she imagined that Colonel Orloff was waiting to advise her as to what she ought to do in regard to the war and to the necessity of putting an end to it as soon as possible. But while she believed that none outside the few people she had admitted into her confidence—one of whom was Anna Wyrubewa, and another Sturmer, who was later on to play such an important part in the tragedy of her fall—could guess what she was abcut, Sazonoff began to suspect that it was due to her influence that the Emperor was no longer so amenable to the advice which he ventured to offer. It was partly to put an obstacle in the way of any independent act of the Sovereign that might have been interpreted as not quite loyal in regard to Russia's Allies, that he had suggested the drawing up of the document known by the name of the Treaty of London, in which the Allied Powers engaged themselves not to conclude any individual or separate peace with Germany. He thought, and others did the same, that this would prove the best means to hold together the Entente without exposing it to mutual suspicion. He concluded this pact of his own authority, only acquainting the Czar with what he had done after it had become an accomplished fact.

Nicholas understood for once the significance of his Minister's bold action, but he could not disavow it; therefore he had to make the best of it. But he refrained from telling the Empress of this new complication which would surely interfere with her hopes of a prompt peace, and it was through a letter from her brother that she heard at last what had taken place in London. Her wrath was intense, the more so that her German relatives blamed her for a thing she had known nothing about and for which they tried to make her responsible. Alexandra Feodorowna had never understood what self-control meant, and she gave public vent to her indignation, accusing Sazonoff of having betrayed his Imperial Master's confidence, and vowing that he would be made to repent for this piece of audacity.

The Empress was still smarting under the sense of her personal defeat in a struggle against the people who were trying to control Russian politics and to lead them in a road she strongly objected taking, when the news of the defeat of the Russian army at Tannenberg came like a thunderbolt out of the blue, to stir up all the patriotic feelings of the Russian nation and to put an end to any idea of peace which may have existed in some timorous minds. The Empress had perforce to appear to share the general indignation against the ruthless conduct of Germany, and she had to acknowledge her momentary helplessness to speak what she considered to be the language of reason, and to try to persuade her subjects that it would be to their advantage to abandon their Allies to their fate, and to apply themselves to withdraw their own pawns out of the game.

In these days of suspense Raspoutine turned out to be the greatest comfort in the world to her. For one thing, he made it possible for her to begin again seeking in Berlin inspirations as to the course of conduct she ought to pursue. Thanks to him, Mr. Manassavitch-Maniuloff was persuaded to undertake a journey abroad, during which he was to see the leading political men in Europe and to ascertain their views on the subject of the conduct of the war in general, as well as of its chances of success. Ostensibly it was a newspaper on which he was assistant editor, the *Nowoie Wrémia*, that sent him on this perilous mission. In reality, he started as the agent of the Empress, and he saw several German officials in Stockholm, as well as in Copenhagen, where he spent a few days. He proceeded to London and to Paris, only to lend coloring to what otherwise would have been an impossible trip. When he returned to Russia he brought along with him a whole program drawn out by the Kaiser, which Alexandra Feodorowna proceeded at once to execute.

But here again she found obstacles in her path, the principal of which was the stubbornness of the Grand-Duke Nicholas, who, in spite of the fact that he had to acknowledge that Russia had neither guns nor ammunition in sufficient quantity to be able to hold her own against the hordes of William II., yet refused to consider his country as beaten. The Grand Duke was popular in the army. The fact that it began to be known that he represented at Court the Russian party, in opposition to the hated Empress, who was supposed to head the German one, gave him considerable prestige. When the Czar had consulted him as to what ought to be done, he had replied:

"Do anything you like except conclude peace, because if you do I shall be the first one to lead the army against you, and to compel you to go on with the struggle."

Nicholas had repeated to the Czarina the threat of his cousin, and this had been sufficient to incense the latter, even more than she had been before, against a man whom she considered, perhaps not quite without reason, as her most formidable enemy.

Nevertheless, she tried to persuade him to change his mind, and made an appeal to his feelings of humanity, asking him whether it was right to go on with a war in which hundreds of thousands of Russian soldiers had already fallen, which would probably entail more sacrifices in the future than the country could afford. She spoke eloquently, but the Grand Duke remained unmoved, and at last Alexandra Feodorowna, worn out by the supreme effort which she had made, gave way to her uncontrollable grief, exclaiming in her deep distress:

"My country, my poor country, must I forsake thee?"

Nicholas Nicholaievitch turned round and said, with a withering contempt:

"To what country do you allude, Madam—to Russia or to Germany?"

The Empress jumped up, her eyes blazing with rage. She rang the bell, and told the lady in waiting who came in response to her call:

"Show the Grand Duke out. He must never be allowed to enter this room any more."

And Nicholas Nicholaievitch never did so again.

CHAPTER XX

IT IS YOUR HUSBAND WHO IS LOSING THE THRONE OF YOUR SON

THIS interview with the Grand Duke, Commander-in-chief of the armies in the field, could not fail to produce a deep impression on the troubled mind of the Empress. Her proud and unforgiving character had been goaded to the extreme by the irony with which her husband's cousin had received the overtures which she had made to him, and she could not bring herself to forgive him for the calm disdain with which he had asked her whether she considered Russia or Germany as her Fatherland.

Of course she flew to Anna Wyrubewa to seek consolation, but when the latter advised her to ask Raspoutine to pray for her in this crisis of her life, Alexandra Feodorowna for once did not accept this suggestion, saying that a man absorbed in religious practices like the "Prophet" could not be expected to take a sane view of a position which was getting so intricate that it would require a statesman of unusual ability to unravel it. But she expressed herself willing to talk to Mr. Sturmer about it, and to ask him what he thought of the Grand Duke's insolence, as she termed it, and what he would suggest as to the means of putting it down.

It is time here to say a word concerning Mr. Sturmer, who was so soon to play a prominent part in the drama of the Romanoffs' fate. He was a man of moderate intelligence, great ambition, and above everything else an opportunist—a perfect type of the class called in Russian Tchinownikis, who always and in everything it does approves the government of the day. He had for years paraded ultra-conservative opinions, and while he had performed the functions of Master of the Ceremonies at the Imperial Court, he had professed great sympathies for England and for everything British, playing the European, while at heart he was the personification of the Tartar hidden under the Russian flag. He was, moreover, an excellent talker and a well-read, well-educated man. His German origin had imbued him, as was to be expected, with considerable admiration for the Kultur, such as it was understood at the time I am referring to. The late Czar Alexander III. had always abominated him and shown him that such was the case in an unmistakable manner. But Mr. Sturmer had the happy knack never to notice what it was inconvenient for him to be caught looking at; he stuck to his post until he contrived to get another appointment, that of President of the zemstwo of the province of Twer, where he possessed a large estate. This position, however, he had to abandon soon, because his colleagues happened all of them to be very ardent liberals who refused to accept his monarchical views.

Sturmer retired to private life, but at the time of the accession to the Throne of Nicholas II. he came to St. Petersburg, and managed to convey to the new Czar a detailed report as to the wave of liberalism that, to use his words, "infected" the province of Twer. If we are to believe a rumor which was persistently circulated in the capital, this had a good deal to do with the famous speech in which the Emperor told the deputies of the zemstwos (come to congratulate him on his marriage) that they need not in the future indulge in "senseless dreams," as it was his firm intention to uphold intact the principles of autocracy.

Sturmer was clever enough to conceal his extreme delight at the Sovereign's attitude, and he went on with his attempt to worm himself into the latter's favor. Very soon afterward he re-entered public life, was appointed Governor of that same province of Twer where he had met with such unsuccess, and proceeded steadily to work out for himself the reputation of being a first-rate statesman. He was shrewd enough to see what others had failed to perceive, and this was that, with the weak character of Nicholas II., it would require very little trouble on the part of the Empress to obtain complete mastery over his mind. He therefore applied himself to persuade the latter that it was her duty to make the attempt. He had always been a fanatical orthodox, perhaps because he had not been born one, and he was in great favor with several high Church dignitaries, including the new confessor of the Imperial Family, Father Schabelsky, whom the Czarina liked very much, and in whom she had great confidence. This made it relatively easy for him to carry to the ears of Alexandra Feodorowna his opinions on the current events of the day, and he did not fail to do so during the troubled times of the Revolution of 1905, and of the repression which followed upon it, in which he took an active part. He occupied then a post in the Ministry. However, he had to give up this upon his appointment as a member of the Council of State, which promotion had covered an attempt on the part of his colleagues to get rid of him. He took an important share in the deliberations of this Assembly, and very soon was recognized as one of the leaders of the ultra-conservative party there, and as a strong supporter of an alliance with Germany.

This attitude alone would have been sufficient to win for him the good-will of the Czarina, and when the war broke out she often talked with him over the sad consequences it was sure to bring; she discussed with this faithful friend the possibility of putting an end to it, in a sense favorable to Russian interests, not likely to harm Russian prestige abroad nor the dynasty at home.

Sturmer had been introduced to Raspoutine by the good offices of Manassavitch-Maniuloff, whose services he had had the opportunity to appreciate when they were both in the employ of the Government, and he soon played a prominent part in all the designs of these two sinister personages. It has even been related that it was due to his special suggestion that the comedy of the Empress being put into direct communication with the spirit of Colonel Orloff had been engineered; of this there exists so far no proof, and we must therefore accept the tale under the reserve that, according to the French proverb, it is only the rich to whom one lends money.

When Sturmer heard about the conversation which had terminated with such violence between Alexandra Feodorowna and the Grand-Duke Nicholas he saw at once the capital that could be made out of the incident. He also disliked the Grand Duke; it was therefore easy for him to enter with alacrity and zeal into the plans of revenge that were being harbored by the Czarina, to whom he reported that Nicholas Nicholaievitch was trying to supplant the Czar, to get himself appointed Dictator of the Empire; that he had, moreover, the most sinister designs against the little Cesarewitsch, as well as against her, who, as he had openly declared, ought to be locked up in a convent. He pointed out further to the distracted Empress that the weakness of character of her husband might easily make him a prey to the ambitions of his cousin and cause him to lend himself to the latter's schemes. Besides this, it was against all the traditions of autocracy for a member of the Imperial Family to aspire to make for himself an independent position outside the Czar, and if the Grand Duke was allowed to work out the consolidation of his popularity among the army and the military party a Palace revolution could easily follow, which would overthrow Nicholas II. and dethrone him in favor of some other Romanoff, willing to become an easy tool in the hands of the Grand-Duke Commander-in-chief.

After this it became the one object of Alexandra Feodorowna's ambition to deprive her cousin of his command, to have him exiled somewhere far from St. Petersburg, which by this time had been renamed Petrograd.

This, however, was a difficult piece of work to perform, precisely on account of the weakness of temperament of Nicholas II. and of the awe with which any violent decision to be taken in regard to any one whom he knew to be stronger than himself inspired him. Religious superstition was therefore brought to bear upon him; he was told by his wife, by a few people who were devoted to her, and last but not least by Raspoutine, that it was part of the duties of a Russian Czar to lead his nation in times of peril; that the enthusiasm which his presence at the head of the army would be sure to provoke would prove a great element in the achievement of a complete victory against a formidable foe, the strength of which had never been properly appreciated. At first Nicholas grew impatient and would not listen. At heart he had the vague consciousness of his own incapacity to command a big army in the field; he feared to take such a perilous responsibility upon his shoulders. He also knew that it was not the fault of the Grand Duke that he had been compelled to retreat before the invading German forces, but of the men who had failed to supply him with the necessary ammunition, artillery, and provisions. The Emperor did not care to make out of his cousin the scapegoat for all the sins of Israel. On the other hand, he dreaded the ascendency which Nicholas Nicholaievitch was undoubtedly acquiring in public opinion, and he did not care for any member of his family to become popular at his own expense. Still, he would not come to a decision. Even when the Grand-Duke Commander-in-chief had objected to the presence of the Empress at headquarters, which she had wished to visit, he had refrained from insisting on the point. He had, on the contrary, applied himself to soothe his wife's ruffled feelings.

This hesitation on the part of the Sovereign did not please at all the small group of men who had entered into the schemes of the Empress. They knew very well that so long as Nicholas Nicholaievitch remained in power it would be impossible to bring to the front the question of a separate peace with Germany for which they were steadily working. It was therefore determined to force the Empress to extort from her husband the decision they wished for; consequently Raspoutine asked her to attend a prayer-meeting he wanted to hold, during which he said that it had been revealed to him that she would come to learn many things hitherto kept from her knowledge, but which it was time she should hear. What occurred at this meeting no one ever could ascertain exactly. It seems pretty certain that Raspoutine evoked the spirit of Colonel Orloff, and that the customary game of making a pencil write by itself was resorted to, with the result that Alexandra Feodorowna returned to the Palace fully convinced that, in resisting her demand for the removal of the Grand-Duke Nicholas from his position as Commander-in-chief of the army, the Czar was endangering not only his own life, but also the Throne, and the chances of succession to it of his only son.

The Empress implored her husband to listen to her, telling him that if he really felt alarmed about taking any violent measures against the Grand Duke, he ought at least to dismiss the latter's head of the staff, General Januchevitch, to whose blunders all the disasters that had overpowered the Russian armies were due. She represented to her bewildered spouse that public opinion claimed some one should be punished for all the unsuccesses which had attended the war, and that it would be satisfied to a small degree if the General were removed from his command.

This was a compromise which Nicholas II. seized hold of with alacrity. It had been proposed to him because it was known very well that the Grand Duke would not consent to be parted from his faithful adviser with whom he had shared all the anxieties of the disastrous campaign that had been carried on amid such terrible difficulties, that he would rather resign his own command than give him up. The surmise proved quite correct. When Nicholas Nicholaievitch was informed of the change that had been made in the direction of the staff, without his having been consulted, he telegraphed to the Emperor, asking him to be also relieved as soon as possible from the duties of his responsible position. The Empress, Sturmer, and Raspoutine were jubilant. It was easy to persuade the Czar that his cousin, in thus resisting his orders, had rendered himself guilty of insubordination. It was decided not to accept his resignation, but simply to dismiss him and to appoint him at the same time Viceroy in the Caucasus, a position that had just been rendered vacant by the departure of Count Worontzoff-Daschkoff for reasons of health. This they thought would be a courteous way of getting rid once for all of a personality so strong and so encumbering at the same time as that of the Grand Duke, and of doing it in a manner to which no one could raise any objections.

The Emperor said yes to everything. He had been thoroughly frightened, and was no longer in a condition of mind capable of judging impartially of the events taking place around him. A solemn religious service was celebrated in the private chapel of the Imperial Palace of Tsarskoye Selo, to implore the protection of Heaven on the new Commander-in-chief of the Russian troops, after which Nicholas II.

started for the headquarters of the army. He was received with great pomp and ceremony by the Grand Duke, and at once assumed the supreme command over demoralized regiments who were full of regret at the departure of their former leader.

Nicholas Nicholaievitch behaved with immense dignity. In this crisis of his life he only remembered that he was a Romanoff, and he showed an absolute submission to the decisions of the head of his dynasty. In words of incomparable nobility he issued an army order in which he thanked his soldiers for their good services, and expressed the hope that the presence of their Sovereign at their head would inspire them with a new energy in the struggle that lay before them. Then he left for his new post, accompanied to the railway station by the Czar himself, from whom he parted solemnly and respectfully, and whom he was never to see again, at least not as Emperor of All the Russias.

The Grand-Duke Nicholas

CHAPTER XXI

PEACE, WE MUST HAVE PEACE

THE removal of the Grand-Duke Nicholas from the position of Commander-in-chief of the army did not meet with the general satisfaction that his enemies had hoped it would provoke. The sane elements of the nation understood quite well that, whatever mistakes he had been guilty of, they had proceeded more from the many difficulties which he had found in his way than from his own incapacity. No one liked the thought of his place having been taken by the Czar himself, who had long ago lost his personal prestige, whom no political party in the country trusted. The influence of the Empress was also dreaded, and the fact of her German leanings was openly discussed. The demand for a responsible Cabinet, from whom explanations could be demanded by the nation, was already to be heard everywhere. The Duma, when it had met, had been the scene of furious discussions during which the conduct of the Government had been severely censured. Russia was beginning to get tired of the tyrannous hand which was weighing it down and crushing every attempt at independence on the part of those who were in possession of her confidence.

The Ministry was neither respected nor considered, the Sovereign was despised, and his wife was hated. Dissatisfaction was spreading even in the spheres which out of old traditions and principles had kept it within bounds. The aristocracy had become weary of finding all its good intentions disdained or misconstrued; in all classes of society people were cursing the hidden "dark powers," as they were called, that disposed of the fate of the nation and that ruled the feeble and weak-minded Monarch who had been converted into a figurehead for whom no one cared except the unscrupulous people who were abusing his credulity and who had contrived to get hold of his confidence.

The Czarina was openly accused of working hand in hand with her cousin, the Kaiser, and of assisting him in his dreams of a world-wide Empire into whose power the Russian one was to be delivered. And when the old, feeble, opinionated, but at any rate honest, Gorémykine had been replaced as Prime Minister by the hated Sturmer, who by this time had risen to the position of leader of the ultra-conservative and reactionary party in the Council of State, the general indignation against the weakness of Nicholas II. could no longer be repressed, and the possibility of a Palace revolution came to be spoken of as the next thing likely to happen.

In the mean while Raspoutine and his friends were daily becoming more powerful. The "Prophet" had by that time completely mastered the details of the intrigue into which he had been drawn by the clever people of whom he had been the tool. These had been at first Count Witte, who in his hatred of the men who had driven him out of power had willingly lent himself to the conspiracy which transformed the Empress into one of the most active agents the Kaiser had ever had at his disposal in Russia. When this much-discussed statesman died at the very moment he might have been called again to play a part in the history of his country, his place had been taken by Sturmer, Manassavitch-Maniuloff, and other adventurers of the same kind, all eager to enrich themselves at the expense of their own Fatherland, all of them men who only looked for their personal financial advantage, who remained perfectly indifferent to the disasters which one after the other were crowding upon unfortunate Russia. Germany was clever enough to see through the game played by these sharks and she did not hesitate an instant in buying their services for all that they were worth.

Raspoutine had very accurately taken stock of the mental caliber of the half-demented Czarina, and while carefully avoiding discussing or even touching upon the subject of politics with her, he had contrived to persuade her to trust those so-called statesmen of whom he was but the instrument. As time went on she became more and more anxious to communicate with these spirits of the other world, in whose existence she had been led to believe as firmly as in that of the Divinity itself. Raspoutine, whenever he prayed in her presence, pretended to get into trances during which he told her things which he assured her he did not remember later on, but which he persuaded her he had been inspired by the celestial powers to tell. She was kept by him and by Anna Wyrubewa in a state of semi-hypnotism, which went so far that sometimes she was herself seized with attacks of convulsions bordering on epilepsy, during the long prayers in which she used to spend half of her days and most of her nights. The superstitious fears which had always haunted her were played upon by these clever adventurers whom she had admitted into the secret of her thoughts. She was finally convinced that her duty as a Russian Empress required of her to sacrifice herself for the welfare of her subjects, and to induce her husband to sign a peace that would put an end to the useless and terrible slaughter that had transformed the whole of Russia into one vast churchyard.

She still labored under the illusion that the dynasty was popular and that every decision of the Czar would be received with respect and gratitude by the nation. Though she knew that she was personally disliked, she did not imagine that this dislike extended itself to the Emperor, and she never supposed that, even in regard to her own person, the hatred of which she was the object existed anywhere else than among the aristocratic circles of Petrograd society. In one word, she believed in the power of autocracy, and she worked as hard as she could to consolidate it by getting Nicholas II. to appoint as his Ministers and advisers men who shared her opinions on this point, and who were ready to crush with the greatest vigor and the utmost severity every attempt to shake the prestige and the authority of the Crown.

Of course, the fact that the country was at war made her path most difficult; for this very reason she thought it was indispensable for the safety of the dynasty and of her son that peace should be concluded. She did not care in the least for the secret treaties or obligations Russia had assumed. To her, honor was but a question of opportunism. She set the existence of the Romanoffs before their self-respect. Her German blood made her lose sight of the real interests of her husband and of her children.

Here we must pause a moment and touch upon a point that has been as much discussed as it has remained mysterious to this day. Was Raspoutine a German agent directly employed by the Kaiser to persuade the half-demented Czarina that it was her duty to put an end to the war? Or was he simply the instrument of other people more in possession of the secret of Germany's schemes than himself? Personally I am inclined to believe this second version of his activity. Raspoutine was far too ignorant and uncouth to have been taken into the confidence of William II., but Mr. Sturmer, Mr. Manassavitch-Maniuloff, and Mr. Protopopoff undoubtedly were confidants of the Kaiser. They had been promised, most likely, large sums of money for their co-operation in this vile intrigue, which even after their fall was to be renewed and, as we have unfortunately seen, renewed with success.

I shall not repeat here the story of Mr. Protopopoff's famous journey to Sweden, where he got into direct touch with agents of the German Government. I shall not even return to the subject of the negotiations begun by him and continued by Mr. Sturmer. All this is now a matter of history, and what I am writing here only concerns the personal part played by the Empress in this dark plot, directed against all the Allies of Russia in the war as well as against Russia herself. I am only concerned with Alexandra Feodorowna and her share in the catastrophe which was to send her a captive and an exile to that distant Siberia whither so many innocent people had been banished by her husband.

I wish to explain how it could have become possible for her to be transformed into an active agent of German ambition on the Russian Throne. She was, as we have seen, only half-responsible for her actions. Her intelligence had never been properly balanced and self-control had never been taught her. She had, however, principles, and very strong ones, too, which had stood between her and temptation in the serious sentimental crisis of her life. But this resistance to what perhaps had been the one passion she had known, except her love for her son, had helped to overthrow her mental balance. She had given to God, represented by a Divinity of her own created by her imagination, all the affection she had not been allowed to expend on earth, and full of a spirit of self-sacrifice as stupid as it was devoid of any ground to stand upon. She had fancied that she could work out her personal salvation, together with that of her family and subjects, in restoring to the country whose Empress she happened to be the blessings of a peace that would stop the effusion of blood the thought of which robbed her of sleep at night and repose by day.

She was living in a state which most certainly was bordering on insanity, and she had entirely lost the faculty of discriminating between what was reality and what was a dream. Raspoutine held her in a kind of trance, which was further aggravated by the long fasts to which he obliged her to submit. She was told that she was the victim chosen by the Almighty to expiate all the sins of the Russian Empire, that it was only through constant prayer, combined with all kinds of other mortifications, that she could hope to see restored the peace of her mind and the health of her son. It is probable that she suffered from hallucinations during which she saw, as in a cloud, the rising shapes of soldiers killed in battle, clamoring to her to stop the useless massacres going on in the Polish plains where they had fallen. Is it a wonder that, unconscious of aught else than this condition of self-reproach to which she had been reduced, she tried to end her own sufferings, as well as the misery which had fallen upon her country, by disregarding all the advice she received from her real friends and making the most frantic efforts to induce her husband to accept the peace terms which the Kaiser had more than once caused to be secretly conveyed to him?

Nicholas II. was also weary of the struggle, but he realized better than his wife the impossibility which existed for him of acting independently of his Allies. He had Ministers who, in spite of their respect for his person and authority, would not have hesitated to point out to him the grave consequences which a defection of Russia would mean for the whole cause of the Allied nations, who, after all, had been entangled in this disastrous war because they had rushed to his help and to that of his people.

Sturmer, who had for a short time taken the conduct of Foreign Affairs in his hands, had been compelled to resign, owing to the opposition which he had encountered in the Duma, and especially owing to the masterful speech in which Professor Miliukoff had exposed all the vices and all the crimes of his administration. His retreat had not had for consequence a diminution of his favor or of his influence; he still remained the trusted adviser of both Czar and Czarina. Together with him were working Protopopoff, who pretended that he would be strong enough, with the help of the hundreds, nay thousands of police agents he had at his disposal, to crush every attempt at a revolution; Madame Wyrubewa; and, last but not least, the formidable Raspoutine, whose influence had proved wide enough to cause the postponement of the trial for blackmail of his confederate, Manassavitch-Maniuloff. A bank director from whom he had tried to extort 25,000 rubles had denounced the latter to the military authorities, and, in spite of the angry protest of Mr. Sturmer, whose confidential adviser he had become, he had been imprisoned and sent before a jury.

But even the efforts of these people combined could not move Nicholas II. to act in accordance with their wishes, because, as I have said, he still had Ministers unwilling to betray the country into the hands of its enemies. The head of the Cabinet was Mr. Trepoff, an honest man credited with liberal sympathies, who, at all events, would not lend himself to anything that could be interpreted into the light of a treason of Russia in regard to her Allies. Unfortunately, he could not hold out against the attacks that were directed against him by all the pro-German party, and after he had fallen the latter felt at last free to act as it liked, because Prince Galitzyne, who had accepted the difficult position of Prime Minister in a country already standing on the brink of ruin, was far too timid a man to dare express an opinion of his own, after the Sovereign had once spoken and signified his will to him.

CHAPTER XXII

THE REMOVAL OF THE "PROPHET"

THERE is a well-known Latin proverb which says that the gods begin by depriving of their reason those whom they mean to destroy.

Never was its truth more forcibly illustrated than in the tragedy which brought about the fall of the autocratic system of government under which Russia had been suffering for centuries. Its last representative had incarnated in his person all the follies, the crimes, the mistakes, and the ruthless cruelty of his predecessors. Unlike them, he had not known how to temper them by personal authority or personal sympathy. He was an effeminate, degenerate descendant of strong ancestors; the whole atavism of a doomed race seemed to have become embodied in his weak individuality. If outside catastrophes had not occurred in his reign, it is still likely that he would have been compelled by a revolution of some kind or other to step back into an obscurity out of which he ought never to have emerged, because he was most certainly not able to bear the rays of the "fierce light which beats upon a throne." It is, however, possible that none of those supreme calamities which destroy the independence and self-respect of nations as well as of individuals would have been connected with his name and history. But destiny condemned him to remain forever, in the annals of the world, a living proof of the degeneracy which threatens all royal houses who do not possess sufficient energy to stand in perfect union with their people whenever a trial of some kind comes to threaten their mutual existence.

It would have been hard enough to be branded by the centuries to come as the last of the Romanoffs and as an unworthy Heir of Peter the Great. It was worse than hard for Russia, even more than for Nicholas II., to have to realize that, through stupidity, weakness of character, and an exaggerated opinion of his own power and might, he had been the direct cause of the ruin of his country and the means of plunging it into an abyss of distress and of anarchy from which it will take the work of several generations to redeem it.

His wife was the instrument of his destruction. About this last point there cannot exist any doubt whatever. She had a character stronger than his and she could speak to him in the name of the son to whom they were both so completely devoted. She could also appeal to his religious and superstitious feelings, which, though not as exaggerated as her own and not quite so foolishly carried to extremes, were yet also devoid of sound common sense. They were connected with the conviction that he had a mission to perform in regard to the future of his subjects, and to their welfare both in this world and in the next. Nicholas II. had in his character something of the traits of Caligula and other Roman emperors—a mixture of cruelty and theatrical sentimentality combined with cowardice in presence of danger and indecision before immediate peril. He never knew what it meant to play the game, and he perished because he refused to fight it out on the day that he discovered his adversary held all the trumps.

In the mean while the war was going on, claiming every day new victims. The insufficiency of the Government to face its various problems became more patent. Instead of applying himself to the task of coping with them, the Czar became absorbed, thanks to the remonstrances of his wife, in the one thought of how to consolidate his own authority, reduce to silence the protestations of the country and those of its representatives in the Duma, and conclude a peace with Germany which would allow him to make an appeal to his troops to help him to crush once more the Revolution which was hammering at his door, which he imagined he could subdue as easily as he had annihilated the one that had broken out after the Japanese campaign.

These were splendid plans indeed, and the Empress was already rejoicing at their success, in ignorance of the revolt which was shaking public opinion out of its previous apathy, a revolt which had extended itself to her own family. Bad as were most of the Grand Dukes, dissolute as their conduct had ever been, yet they had in their veins the blood of Catherine the Great and of all the dead and gone Romanoffs. They rose in rebellion against the gang of adventurers who were dishonoring the chief of their race and of their dynasty.

By that time the name of the Empress was being dragged in the dirt by every street boy, and open comments were made in public places in regard to her friendship, not to call it by another name, for Raspoutine—comments which were devoid of truth, because there was never any immorality in their relations, but which were generally believed, perhaps, because it would have been impossible for any one to guess that it was through superstitious practices that the "Prophet" had contrived to get absolute hold of her mind.

The Imperial Family felt the degradation to which this common peasant had reduced it, and though they had no reason in the world to like Nicholas II., yet they resented the humiliation which any slur upon the reputation of his wife conferred upon him as well. After all, Alexandra Feodorowna was the mother of the future Czar, and as such she ought to inspire respect in the Russian nation. If she did not realize this fact herself, others had to do it for her and rid her of a contact which was a slur. Besides, there was the hope that if once the adventurer was removed she could be brought to look upon the world from a more reasonable point of view. The principal thing was to deliver her from this evil adviser who was fast leading her, as well as the dynasty, to inevitable destruction and ruin.

The story of Raspoutine's assassination is too well known to be repeated here. At any time it would have broken the heart of the poor, misguided Czarina. But coming at the moment it took place, it did something more—it deprived her of what she considered to be her only moral support amid the troubles of her life, the possibility of communicating with the spirit of the man whom she had loved, who she felt sure was watching over her and over her child, from the heavens.

In the weeks preceding the murder of the "Prophet" he had subjected the Empress almost every evening to the agony of these prayer-meetings during which he communicated to her the so-called wishes of her dead friend, who, as he said, advised her, through his medium, as to what she ought to do to avert the dangers which were hovering over her head. The miserable woman used to listen to these revelations with anxious eagerness, and pray, pray, with a fervor she had never known before, for the strength to obey the commandments of a spirit who in death, as well as in life, had proved to be her best, and indeed her only, friend. Is it a wonder that the last remnants of sanity which were still left to her snapped under this terrible strain, and that at last she became the mere shadow of her former self, a fit subject for a lunatic asylum, where, indeed, she ought, for the good of everybody, to have been confined?

Her conduct after she had been told of the murder of the creature whom she revered as a Prophet of God was quite in accord with her character, such as it had developed itself through all the years during which she had allowed her mind to be invaded with superstitious notions, which would have been laughable if they had not been so pathetic. Her only thought was that of vengeance. She exercised it with a relentlessness which set against her the few people left in Petrograd who might have felt inclined to take her part and to pity her in this tragedy of her life. She left no peace for the Czar until he had exiled the persons whom she knew to have been the authors of the deed. When she was implored to take pity on the young Grand-Duke Dmitry, and not have him sent to the Persian front, where there existed so many epidemics that it was hardly likely he would ever come back again, she had merely smiled and coldly said:

"Why should I pity him? He did not pity others."

And yet public feeling was so strong against her, and so entirely in favor of those who had had the courage to rid Russia of a man who had proved so fatal to it, that the schemes of revenge of Alexandra Feodorowna suffered a collapse. Mighty and powerful as Nicholas II. believed himself to be, yet he understood that the best thing he could do would be to let silence and oblivion fall over a crime that was eminently popular in the whole country. He had heard of the telegrams of congratulation, and of the flowers which had been sent to both his cousin Dmitry Pawlowitch and to the husband of his niece, young Prince Youssoupoff, as well as the joy to which the population of Petrograd had given way when it had become aware of the fate of the adventurer whose name had been so prominently and so sadly associated with that of the Empress of All the Russias. Perhaps at heart he was not so very sorry at an event which had certainly rid him of a great incumbrance.

Nicholas II. had always practised dissimulation to a considerable extent, and he had never allowed outsiders to guess what was going on in his mind. During the days which followed upon the disappearance of Raspoutine he certainly expressed great sympathy for the grief of his wife, but at the same time he did not, as she expected, cause the perpetrators of the murder of this low adventurer to be prosecuted publicly for their daring action. This apathy exasperated Alexandra Feodorowna.

During the last weeks of Raspoutine's life he had been working, conjointly with Sturmer and Protopopoff, toward convincing her to lend herself to a Palace revolution which would have overturned her husband and made little Alexis Czar under her own Regency. She had been told over and over again that she possessed all the great talents of Catherine II., that the Emperor was not a better man than Peter III. She had been made acquainted with his unpopularity, but at the same time persuaded that this unpopularity was a purely personal thing and that it did not extend itself to the person of the Heir to the Throne, nor even to her own. As Regent she could do any amount of good, and conclude peace with Germany the more easily that she was not bound by the terms of the agreement entered into by Mr. Sazonoff with the Entente, in the name of Nicholas II.

The foolish woman believed absolutely all the nonsense which was being constantly poured into her ears. Her ambition and lust for revenge over her enemies also played a part in this whole tragedy. She therefore began wondering whether, after all, she ought not to follow the advice which she had received from Heaven, as she fondly imagined, through the mouth of Raspoutine. She would have liked to be able to consult once again the spirit of Colonel Orloff so as to relieve her perplexity, because she had still sufficient scruples to hesitate before allowing those whom she considered to be her friends to use her name for the execution of a Palace revolution directed against her own husband, whom she may not have loved, but whom she still respected as the Czar of All the Russias.

It is at this juncture that a new incident occurred, the real details of which have never yet transpired. Raspoutine, just before he had been murdered, had introduced to the Empress a Tibetan doctor with whom he was on terms of intimate friendship, telling her that he was a man of great ability, devoted to occult sciences, had studied them in the convents of his country, and who was quite able to perform miracles. This man, whose name was Badmaieff, certainly saw Alexandra Feodorowna several times, and it was reported that he gave her certain drugs which he told her she ought to administer to the Emperor in secret, drugs which would make him quite subservient to her will. Whether she used them or not it is impossible to say. Young Prince Youssoupoff declared immediately after the Revolution that she had done so, and that in consequence of this experiment Nicholas II.'s will, which had always been a weak one, had completely disappeared, until he had been reduced to the condition of a puppet in the strong hands of his wife. But this assertion, coming as it did from a personage who could not have nursed kind feelings in regard to the Empress, must be accepted with caution.

It is a fact, however, that those in attendance on the Sovereign remarked more than once that he seemed at times to have lost the real consciousness of what was going on around him, that his eyes had acquired a vague, dazed look they had never worn before.

It is out of this introduction of Badmaieff into the intimacy of the Czarina that the rumor arose that Raspoutine, together with Anna Wyrubewa, had tried to administer slow poison to the small Grand-Duke Alexis. Such a thing had never taken place, and indeed it could never have occurred if one considers the fact that the strongest trump in the game played by the pro-German agents who were leading Russia to its ruin was precisely the little Cesarewitsch, without whose existence it would have been impossible for them to think of making out of Alexandra Feodorowna a Regent of the Russian Empire. They had, therefore, the greatest interest in keeping the child in as good a state of health as possible, and he was far too delicate for them to try any experiment upon him. On the other hand, the necessity of getting rid by natural means of the Czar himself was so evident that it would not be surprising if the superstitious mind of his Consort had been influenced so as to persuade her to lend herself to what she had been told was nothing but a religious practice, but which in reality was an attempt to accomplish by this means what it would perhaps not have proved wise to try and bring about in another way.

CHAPTER XXIII

ANNA COMES TO THE RESCUE

IN the course of an interview which Anna Wyrubewa gave to a foreign newspaper correspondent a short while after she had been released from the fortress of SS. Peter and Paul, where she was confined for about three months following the outbreak of the Revolution, she said that the Empress Alexandra had never been so near to insanity as during the weeks which followed upon the murder of Raspoutine. What she failed to relate, however, was the manner in which she succeeded in preventing the half-balanced mind of the miserable woman from snapping altogether under the strain put upon it by circumstances.

When the outsider tries to form an opinion as to all the events which preceded the rebellion that destroyed the Throne of the Romanoffs, it is essential he should remember the state of mind of the Czarina at this particular time, as well as the condition of her nerves—a condition which was very nearly akin to the one into which a man falls when, after having been the victim of a pernicious drug habit, he finds himself unexpectedly and suddenly deprived of his favorite morphia or cocaine. The Empress had been living for months under the influence of these mysterious night sittings during which Raspoutine evoked for her, as she firmly believed, spirits of another world from whom she sought inspiration and in whom she found comfort. All at once this moral aid, which had helped her to live, was denied to her, and she did not know any longer what she was to do, surrounded as she felt herself to be by ever-increasing dangers which threatened not only her own person, but that of her beloved child, that son in whom she firmly believed Russia would find its salvation and who was destined to become one of the greatest and mightiest Sovereigns the country had ever seen reign over it since the days of Peter the Great. She felt absolutely at sea, like a ship deprived of its pilot and abandoned to inexperienced hands, ignorant of the first principles of navigation. Neither her husband, whom at heart she despised, nor her friend, Anna Wyrubewa, whom she had never entirely initiated into all the details of her secret intercourse with the dead, nor her faithful advisers, Sturmer and Protopopoff, could make up to her for the irreparable loss of the companionship which, thanks to Raspoutine, she believed she had succeeded in establishing between herself and the soul of the only man she had ever truly loved.

It is only after having grasped these essential facts in the life of the misguided Empress of Russia that it is possible to come to a reasonable appreciation of her person, character, and intrigues.

Once this has been done, it becomes relatively easy to understand the influence which Raspoutine had acquired over her mind, and not to share the general opinion that there existed something immoral in her relations with him. Immorality alone could not explain this entire submission on the part of a cultured, well-educated, elegant woman to the will of a dirty, uncouth, ignorant peasant. Besides that, Alexandra Feodorowna was far too proud to forget for one moment the social difference which separated her from the "Prophet." In her intercourse with him she remained the Empress, and on his side he was far too shrewd not to remember it also. He knew very well that one indiscreet word, one imprudent gesture, would have put an end at once to his influence, and the man as well as his accomplices were working for far too great and far too important an object to compromise its success by anything which might have savored of immoral intrigue.

The state of health of the little Cesarewitsch also was not the real reason why the latter's mother would not allow Raspoutine to leave her. She believed in the efficacy of his prayers for her son, but this belief alone would not have been sufficient to make her so entirely submissive to his will and to reduce her to the state of slavery into which she had been entranced. No, the secret of Raspoutine's influence lay in the simple fact that, thanks to the hypnotic faculties which he undoubtedly possessed, he had contrived to acquire an absolute dominion over her mind, and to persuade her that every time she prayed with him she was put into direct communication with her dead lover; that this lover had been allowed by the Almighty to come to her help in the troubles and perplexities of her life, to guide her in her conduct as a woman and a mother and in her duties as a Sovereign.

During the hours of agony which followed upon the news of the murder of that man whom she had considered as a holy creature and a real Prophet of God, Alexandra Feodorowna blurted out something of what lay on her mind to her devoted friend and companion, Anna Wyrubewa. The latter had removed from her own house to the Palace of Tsarskoye Selo, so as to be able to remain in constant attendance on the miserable Empress. Seeing her so forlorn and desolate, she bethought herself of rousing her faculties, and tried to persuade her that, though she had lost her advisers and counselors, she had yet a duty to perform, which consisted in going on with the work they had suggested to her to start. Peace was more than ever necessary to Russia, as well as to the dynasty, against which such fierce attacks were being launched. The sacred principles of autocracy that were being everywhere challenged ought to be maintained, and how could this be done when the army which was the only force on which the Czar could rely was being kept at the frontier and uselessly butchered in battles it could not by any possibility win? There were other mothers besides herself in Russia who were crying over their dead sons and appealing to her to spare those who were still left to them. This war was a monstrous crime against humanity, as well as against the whole of the Russian nation. It must be stopped because otherwise worse calamities even than those that had already fallen on the country would occur. The performance of a duty was sometimes painful, but this ought not to prevent any right-minded person from trying to accomplish it. It was quite evident that the duty of the Empress required her to work toward the conclusion of peace with Germany, and this had been already suggested to her not only by the devoted friends she still had in the world, but by the spirit of the dead ones who had loved and honored her while they had been alive on earth.

The Cesarewitsch

Whether Anna Wyrubewa was sincere or not in thus pleading a cause which she knew her Imperial mistress had but too much at heart even without her interference, I shall not attempt to guess. Russia was most certainly going through a terrible crisis, and those who thought that the quick conclusion of a peace after which so many were secretly longing and sighing was indispensable were by no means a small minority in the country. It is quite likely that the Empress's confidante was sincere in her conduct, and it seems pretty certain that she had no pecuniary or material advantages in view when she lent herself to the dangerous scheme suggested to her by Sturmer and the latter's accomplices. *They* were not disinterested; they had decidedly ambitious views as to their own future, and they were most certainly in the employ of Germany, to which they had promised their co-operation. Protopopoff was a man who, in regard to the large fortune he was credited with possessing, was entirely self-made; he had never shown any hesitation as to the choice of the means by which he had acquired it. Sturmer thought himself endowed with the genius of a Bismarck or of a Richelieu, and dreamed of the glory of a peace that would leave Russia in appearance as strong as ever, but united by the closest of ties to the German Empire, of which he had been all through his political career a devoted admirer and servant. He had always preached the necessity of the renewal of the former alliance that in bygone times had united the Hohenzollerns and the Romanoffs. His vanity felt deeply flattered upon hearing from his friends in Berlin that the Kaiser, as well as the latter's Government, considered him the one great Minister Russia had ever possessed and were looking up to him to heal all the evils and all the miseries which the war had brought about. He did not care for the treaties that had been signed between Russia and her Allies, and probably shared the opinion of Mr. von Bethmann-Hollweg that all such documents were nothing but scraps of paper, not worthy of any notice on the part of intelligent people. He cared only for success, for titles, decorations, power, and a crowd of flatterers about him. Russia had ceased to be for him a matter for consideration. She would always fare well, in his opinion, if only he were allowed to direct her destinies. The war itself, with all the terrible breakage it had brought about, did not trouble him. It had begun with broken treaties and broken faith, broken honor and broken word; its result had been broken houses in broken lands, broken men, and broken hearts, but about these last Mr. Sturmer did not think at all.

And what about the third personage in this sinister tragedy? What about Manassavitch-Maniuloff, who had been all along the *Deus ex machina* of this dark intrigue, and the chief spy and accomplice of William II.? It was he who had engineered the conspiracy for peace which was being carried on by the Empress under his supervision. It was he who had been the real creator of the Raspoutine legend, and he was perhaps the one who at first suffered the most through the collapse of the adventurer. When the "Prophet" was murdered, Maniuloff was in prison under the accusation of blackmail. Once before he had escaped a trial that had been postponed on the personal order of Nicholas II. addressed to the president of the court. But after Raspoutine's disappearance the influence of Sturmer alone had not been able to help him. He was sent before a jury and sentenced to two years' penal servitude, which, however, he was never to undergo. The man had more than one arrow to his bow, and when the Revolution broke out he contrived to let Kerensky know that he could put at his disposal most incriminating documents in regard to the part played by the Empress in the peace negotiations which had taken place in the preceding February between Petrograd and Berlin. The bait probably took, because the spy who had for a long number of years cheated everybody was sent across the frontier to expiate his sins and most probably to go on for the benefit of the new masters of Russia with the nefarious game he had been playing in regard to all those who had had the misfortune to employ him.

After Sturmer had been compelled to resign his position of Prime Minister and leader of the Foreign Office he had, nevertheless, remained, as I have had already the occasion to tell, in close relations with the Court and with the Emperor and Empress. He had acquired a new ally in the person of the Metropolitan of Petrograd, Monseigneur Pitirim, a friend and favorite of Raspoutine, who now came to offer his consolations to the half-distracted Alexandra, and who also told her that it was henceforward her duty to go on doing all that the dead "Prophet" had suggested to her, no matter how much it might cost her. Between his preachings, the advice of Sturmer and Protopopoff, and the adjurations of Anna Wyrubewa, the Empress was at last persuaded to forget for a while the deep grief into which she had allowed herself to fall and to resume her political activity. But when she attempted to influence the Czar to approve of what she was about to do she found, to her surprise, that he did not show the same enthusiasm for her schemes as he had done before.

What had happened was this: The Imperial Family had once more tried to open the eyes of the Sovereign as to the folly of his wife's conduct. Nearly all the Grand Dukes and Grand Duchesses in Petrograd had sought his presence in succession, implored him to save the dynasty before it was too late, and to call together a responsible Ministry, chosen from among the men who had the confidence of the country and who represented it in the Duma. Their remonstrances had not convinced Nicholas II., but they had caused him to pause before consenting to the conclusion of a peace with Germany, which he began to fear he would not have the power or the strength to impose upon public opinion in Russia. He believed in his wife, and he felt convinced that she was the only disinterested friend left to him; at the same time he could not make up his mind to take a decision which—this much he knew—would be deeply resented by his Allies as well as by his own subjects. In his perplexity he preferred to wait for events to develop themselves in one sense or in the other, totally oblivious of the fact that there are periods in the life of nations when waiting is also a crime.

And while this struggle was going on in his mind, that of his wife was becoming more and more the prey of the evil advisers who had secured her sympathies and were abusing her confidence. They were becoming bolder and bolder as time went on, and at last they suggested to her to urge upon the Czar the necessity of returning to the front, where, they told her, he could come to a better understanding of the feelings of the army and be at last convinced that it was, like the rest of Russia, only longing for peace. Nicholas caught eagerly at the suggestion and departed, leaving the Empress mistress of the field and free to do what she liked, together with her friends.

CHAPTER XXIV

YOU MUST BECOME THE EMPRESS

WHEN the Czar left Tsarskoye Selo—for the last time, as it turned out, as a powerful, dreaded Sovereign—the Empress had not yet made up her mind as to what she ought to do. She was being urged by Sturmer and Protopopoff to come to a decision in regard to the future of the dynasty, which they declared to her was entirely in her hands; at the same time she lacked the moral courage to put herself boldly at the head of a movement to dethrone her husband. She had not the audacity of Catherine the Great, nor the latter's unscrupulousness, and, moreover, her mind was so weakened by the superstitious practices in which she had become absorbed that it is to be questioned whether or not she was given a true account of what was going on around her. She was entirely at the mercy of the first determined man who came along, audacious enough to compel her to sing according to his tune. But neither Sturmer nor Protopopoff were clever enough to be that. And they had no political party on whom they could rely to help them execute any plans they might form. They depended for their inspiration on the directions which they received from Berlin. By a lucky accident this inspiration failed them at the very moment they most needed it.

What had happened was this: The Allies had begun to get some inkling as to the intrigue which was going on under the Czar's own roof, an intrigue in which his wife held the foremost rôle. They contrived to put obstacles in the way of Mr. Protopopoff and of his friends, and to stop for a while the active correspondence which he was carrying on with the German Government *via* Stockholm. At the same time they arranged matters in such a way that the liberal leaders in the Duma became apprised of the negotiations pending between the Kaiser and his kinswoman at Tsarskoye Selo.

The story of the eventful days which preceded the Revolution have nothing to do with the present book, and I shall refer to them only in so far as they concern the Empress. She was mostly responsible for the rapidity with which rebellion spread and for the unexpected way in which it broke out. Had she remained quiet, it is likely that things might have dragged on for a few weeks, perhaps even for a few months, longer, because no one at this particular moment cared to see a change in the Government. But when it was ascertained that she had become a danger to the nation in general there was no longer any question of a delay, and events had to be forced on in some way or other.

What Sturmer proposed to the Czarina was to provoke a movement against the war in the garrisons of Petrograd and the towns in its neighborhood; this to be further accentuated by false news concerning the Czar, who would be represented as having died suddenly. The Government had at its disposal all the telegraph and telephone wires. It was, therefore, an easy matter to cut off the capital from all communication with the headquarters of the army. In the confusion inseparable from the consternation caused by the news of the Sovereign's demise it would have been but a matter of a few hours to get the little Grand-Duke Alexis proclaimed Emperor under the Regency of his mother, who would thus have been left free to sign a peace which nothing and no treaty prevented *her* from concluding. Nicholas would be easily persuaded to accept accomplished facts and most likely would surrender with pleasure, or at least with absolute indifference, a Throne he had never cared for. So they thought that an act of formal abdication would not be difficult to obtain from him.

The country also would not feel sorry to be rid of a Monarch who had never been in possession of its affection or respect, and the army, glad to return to its homes, would most likely rally with alacrity around the Regent and the little Czar. The very fact that it was a woman and a delicate child upon whom the whole burden of an immense responsibility had fallen would predispose public opinion in their favor, and most likely this Palace revolution would end with complete success.

The Empress allowed herself to be won over to the conspiracy, and it was decided to put it into execution about the middle of the month of February. Protopopoff declared that he required that much time to gather together a sufficient number of police agents in Petrograd, without whom he did not dare to risk the adventure. Alexandra Feodorowna assented to everything that was proposed to her. She went about like one in a dream, unconscious of the abominable plot in which she had been induced to participate, thinking only of the time when she would be able at last to renew with her own family and with her own people the tender and intimate relations which the war had forcibly interrupted.

In the mean time the Emperor remained at the front, and if we are to believe all that was subsequently related about his conduct there, he changed considerably his opinion and point of view after having resumed direct contact with his troops. He convinced himself that they were not at all as anxious for peace as he had been led to expect, and that the feelings of the men in regard to Germany were revengeful more than anything else. His generals, and especially Aléxieieff, who was Head of the Staff, kept urging upon him the necessity of preparing a formidable offensive, this time on the Riga front. The General gave him hopes that it would turn out to be a successful one, provided (and this was the one everlasting and burning question) that the War Office sent sufficient ammunition to the front. The Emperor was persuaded that this could be done, but Aléxieieff was not so sanguine, and he started a private inquiry of his own as to what was going on in Petrograd in that respect. The result of it was that he was convinced that the Ministry had lately completely neglected this important item and had spent its time in arresting workmen whom it suspected of harboring democratic opinions, as well as in curtailing the hours of labor at the different factories where ammunition was manufactured.

Protopopoff wanted the war to end, and he hoped that in limiting the output of shells and guns he would be able to place the country in such a position that a cessation of hostilities would become unavoidable.

A report to the Emperor, in which the situation such as it presented itself was exposed with great details, was brought to him by the Staff. As usual, it left him unmoved. He merely said that he would give orders to the War Office to take henceforward its orders from the Commander-in-chief of the Armies in the Field, meaning himself, but he refused to blame Protopopoff or to hear anything concerning the appointment of a liberal and responsible Cabinet from whom the Duma could require accounts. He did not mean to lessen his own prerogatives by the merest fraction, and he still thought that Russia might hold its own against her formidable foes without arms, provisions, shells, or big guns, and in general without means of defense capable of stopping the progress of the invaders in their triumphal march through his Empire.

The commanders of the different fronts held a consultation, and one of them, whose name I cannot mention at the present moment, first suggested the idea that it would not be a bad thing to try and bring about a military conspiracy which would overthrow the weak Monarch whom it was impossible to bring to take a sane view of the position in which the army found itself placed. Another general suggested that such an upheaval would only bring to the foreground the personality of the Empress, who would insist on being consulted in all matters in which the welfare of her son might be concerned. And no one wanted Alexandra Feodorowna to be raised to a position in which her voice might come to exercise an influence of any kind on the destinies of the country. It was by far preferable to let Nicholas II. remain where he was, and try to persuade him to allow the Staff, instead of the Cabinet, to have the last word to say in all questions connected with the national defense.

This secret, or rather not secret, conference, because its purport became known on the very same day it took place, thus accomplished nothing. In the mean while the object of its deliberations was communicated to the Ministry in Petrograd, and Protopopoff triumphantly informed the Empress of the fact that it had come to almost the same conclusions which he and his friends had arrived at long before. It was necessary to change the person of the Sovereign. He carefully refrained, however, from acquainting her with the knowledge of the opposition that the idea of a Regency had provoked.

It is a curious but certain fact that at this very time large sums of money were distributed to the troops quartered in Petrograd, Tsarskoye Selo, Peterhof, and Gatschina by unknown people in the name of the Empress. The latter declared, later on, when questioned on the subject by the Provisional Government, that she had known nothing about it; certainly it had not been her money which had been scattered about with such reckless generosity. I believe that in saying so she spoke the absolute truth. But then the question arises, by whose orders was this money thrown into the arena of the battle-field, where the fate of a nation and of a dynasty was about to be decided? Some people have declared that it was Protopopoff together with Sturmer who had hit upon the idea of making Alexandra Feodorowna popular among the army by appearances of a generosity with which no one had credited her before. But against this theory comes the probability that if either of the above-mentioned gentlemen had been able to draw from the Treasury several millions of rubles to be applied to secret purposes, they would have begun by putting them into their own pockets and trusting to the future and to Providence for the success of any enterprise they embarked upon. Therefore the question arises again as to the origin of this money which was circulated with such a generous hand among the regiments considered as likely to lend themselves to a Palace revolution in favor of the delicate little boy who was the sole Heir to all the glory and the splendor of the Romanoffs.

I think that very few people, among those who knew how vital was Germany's interest at this particular moment to see a peace concluded, will doubt whence came these funds. They were certainly spent to favor the appointment of the Czarina as Regent of the Russian Empire. Who had procured them for the benefit of a vast conspiracy, the object of which was to deliver Russia, bound hand and foot, to the tender mercies of her formidable neighbor and enemy?

On the other hand, the liberal parties, now thoroughly awakened to the dangers of the situation, were also working earnestly toward the defeat of the plans conceived by Messrs. Sturmer, Protopopoff & Co. Several meetings of the leaders of the different factions in the Duma took place at the Tauride Palace, but none seemed to come to anything serious in the way of a revolution, which had been by that time recognized as absolutely inevitable.

The Cabinet saw this hesitation, and would undoubtedly have struck a serious blow at its adversaries if, just at the time, the children of the Empress had not sickened from the measles in a serious form. The mother forgot all her political intrigues in her anxiety; the plot about to be executed had perforce to be put off until a more favorable day. It must be here remarked that the Czar, when he heard about his son's and daughters' illness, telegraphed to his wife asking her whether she wished him to come back to Tsarskoye Selo. This did not suit in the least the people who were only waiting for a favorable opportunity to dethrone their Sovereign. Alexandra Feodorowna was easily persuaded to oppose herself to this desire of her husband and to wire back to him not to return. By a singular coincidence the presence of Nicholas II. at Tsarskoye Selo, which would without doubt have given quite another coloring to events which were going to happen within a few days, was desired neither by his friends nor by his foes nor even by his family. They all of them knew that something terrible was about to take place, but they also felt that, for the sake of everybody, it would be better he should be absent.

And in the silence of his study at Potsdam the Kaiser was secretly discounting this Russian Revolution which he saw quite clearly was approaching with quickening strides. He knew what he was about, and little did it matter to him if those whom he had used as pawns in the difficult game he had been playing would perish or not in the storm which his efforts had contributed to let loose.

CHAPTER XXV

THE NATION WANTS YOUR HEAD

I FEEL personally sure—and others who were in Petrograd at the time of the fall of the Romanoffs told me the same thing—that in this whole history of the overthrow of one of the most formidable powers the world had ever known there are yet details which we do not know. In fact, no one knows them, but perhaps they will be explained to us later on. The catastrophe occurred with such startling rapidity that even those who were the most concerned in it were hardly able to realize its importance, even while recognizing its seriousness.

There is also another curious feature connected with the tragedy. All its principal actors, the men who were really instrumental in bringing about the change which transformed Russia from an autocratic—the most autocratic Government in the world, in fact—into a democratic Republic disappeared before even their task was done. It was the Duma in the person of its president, Mr. Rodzianko, it was the zemstwos who had taken up the cause of the liberal movement from the very beginning of the war, who really were responsible for the abdication of Nicholas II. And yet the Duma disappeared, melted into space with an unbelievable rapidity; Mr. Rodzianko has hardly been heard of since the activity of the zemstwos was suddenly interrupted.

How did all this happen? Who was responsible for the chaos into which Russia is plunged at the present moment? It is next to impossible to say to-day, though one may easily guess. All that the world knows is that chaos has supervened, and that, thanks to this chaos, Germans have once more re-entered Petrograd, by the back door, perhaps, but still re-entered it, and what does this detail matter to them! What they wanted was only to get there again; the rest would adjust itself as time went on, and the general confusion became even more complete than it was at the beginning.

Another feature in this extraordinary Revolution was the swiftness with which the country accepted it and accommodated itself to its consequences. In the space of a few hours the portraits of the Czar had disappeared from all public places, the Imperial arms, wherever these had graced a shop or concern of some kind, had followed suit. Ushers in the former Imperial theaters had discarded their liveries, sentinels at the Winter Palace had been removed, and the Red flag had taken the place of the Romanoff standard on top of the Imperial Residence. All this had been performed quietly, joyously, and in a perfectly orderly manner. It seemed almost as if people had been prepared for a long time for what was to come and had practised beforehand the various manifestations of their joy to which they gave vent as soon as it became known that the Guard regiments quartered in the capital had gone over to the Duma and sworn allegiance to Mr. Rodzianko, its president.

Of the war there was no longer any question. It seemed to be forgotten in the excitement of the hour, and somehow a general impression prevailed that, once the Czar had been overturned, peace was but a question of days. By one of those strange anomalies such as happen so often in life, the Czar had been accused of wishing to bring this peace about; yet when he was no longer there the world rejoiced at the thought that peace would surely be concluded before any unreasonable quantity of water had run through the Neva. It is also a singular feature of this singular time that while Petrograd was in the throes of revolution, while Ministers with Mr. Protopopoff at their head were being arrested and transferred to the fortress, the Czar at headquarters and the Empress at Tsarskoye Selo did not in the least suspect what was taking place in the capital. It was said later that the Grand-Duke Paul had forced his way into the apartments of Alexandra Feodorowna and had acquainted her with the details of the upheaval which was to carry away her Throne.

I can hardly bring myself to believe this. For one thing, no one in the Imperial Family cared sufficiently for the Czarina to take the trouble to warn her of any peril in which she might find herself. And then she had not been upon good terms with the Grand-Duke Paul in particular; it is to be questioned if she would, in view of the fact that it was his son who had helped to slay Raspoutine, have consented to receive him in general. I think it far more likely that it was only through the indiscretion of some of her attendants that the Empress heard of what was taking place. It is probable her first thought was that her friends had been working in her behalf, and that the insurrectionary movement which was shaking Petrograd was distinctly in her favor; that its aim was to make out of her the Regent of the Russian Empire.

It would be difficult, otherwise, to understand her apathy in the presence of this overwhelming catastrophe, or the resistance which she opposed to the advice which the few attendants who were still faithful to her and who had remained at Tsarskoye Selo, gave to her—to telegraph immediately to the Czar to return home. Up to the last minute she refused to do so, saying that she felt quite capable of resisting the mob in case it chose to invade the Imperial Residence. And at last it was not she, but the officer in command of the troops quartered in the town, who took it upon himself to inform General Woyeikoff, head of the Okhrana, or personal police service of the Czar, that it was high time for the Sovereign to return home, as he could no longer guarantee the safety of the Empress and of her children. All the regiments under his orders had gone over to the enemy.

Alexandra Feodorowna was waiting the whole time for Protopopoff and Sturmer; she was only wondering why they were so long in coming to her. When at last she was informed that they had been arrested by the mob and taken to the fortress, whither they had sent so many innocent people, she began to realize that things were not going so smoothly as she had fondly imagined, that something quite out of the common had taken place. Then she remembered certain words which Raspoutine had told her: so long as he was at her side no harm would befall her, but that, if he were once removed, misfortune upon misfortune would crowd on the House of Romanoff and sweep away the Crown to which she had become so attached.

In that acute moment when there flashed across her mind this prediction of a man in whom she had seen a Prophet of the Almighty, and the Empress realized the tragedy of her destiny, all the courage of which she had boasted earlier fell flat to the ground. She no longer thought of struggling against an implacable fate, and a complete indifference as to her possible future took the place of her previous energy and determination. The game was lost, absolutely lost, and she had better confess herself beaten before any more harm was done.

News of her husband's abdication reached her, and did not even rouse her sentiments of revolt at a piece of weakness which, under different circumstances, would have brought on one of those hysterical attacks to which she had been subject. She understood that she was alone, quite alone with the burden of her past sins and mistakes. She accepted with stoical resignation the decrees of Destiny. Not one single feeling of pity for the miserable Monarch for whose fall she was so responsible, or for the children about to lose a glorious inheritance, moved her heart. She was thinking the whole time of the dead man who had loved her and of the murdered adventurer who had comforted her in the hours of her greatest moral agony.

Nothing seemed to make any impression on her blurred mind—not even the angry crowd when it appeared in the courtyard of the Palace where she was still staying, carrying before it great banners upon which were written the ominous words:

"Give us the head of Alexandra Feodorowna! We want the head of that German woman, Alexandra Feodorowna!"

When asked to leave the window and not to appear before this multitude clamoring for her blood, she merely shrugged her shoulders and remained where she was. She certainly was not courageous, but she did not lack bravery—the bravery born of fatalism or of indifference, which renders those who are endowed with it impassible before danger, because they fail to realize its importance or its imminence. This woman is a historical riddle which only history will be able to unravel, but not so soon as one imagines, because it is likely that she has not yet come to the end of her sinister and mischievous career.

While the life of his wife was threatened, while his Ministers were imprisoned, and while the nation was preparing to claim his abdication, Nicholas II., at Mohilew, where headquarters were stationed, remained just as indifferent to the convulsions which were shaking his country as the Empress watching by the bedside of her sick children. He also did not understand; he also failed to realize that what was taking place in Petrograd was the first act of a big game the stakes of which might easily come to be his own head and those of his family. The thought of Louis XVI. never once crossed his mind. At least it is allowed one to suppose so, because, when some officers of his suite remarked to him that the rebellion (the news of which had by that time reached him) bore many traits of resemblance to the premonitory riots that had heralded the introduction of the Terror in France, he simply replied:

"Oh, it is not at all the same thing. Russians are not Frenchmen—and the Romanoffs are not the Bourbons."

The Czar might at this early stage of the Revolution have returned to Tsarskoye Selo if he had only energetically insisted upon doing so. But he spent three days in complete indecision, and when at last he made up his mind to go home it was too late. By that time General Aléxieieff had been won over to the cause of the Duma, which was supposed to represent the only responsible authority in Russia; he put every possible obstacle in his way, going so far as to interfere with the arrangements made by General Woyeikoff for the departure of the Imperial train. It seems also that he sent telegrams asking for this train to be either stopped or at least delayed on its way.

No one at this stage wished Nicholas II. to go back to Petrograd, where it was feared his presence would prevent, if not stop, the establishment of the new Government; a useless fear, because, even if he had reached his former capital, he would never have found sufficient courage or energy to fight against an adverse fate or to do aught else but submit to the will of the multitude eager for his fall. The man who signed without one word of protest an abdication against which his whole soul ought to have protested, such a man was not to be feared, he could only be despised.

This was also the feeling which the whole nation began to entertain for him. People had pitied him in the beginning, but as the details of his conduct at Pskow became known, contempt took the place of any commiseration which the tragedy of his fate might have provoked. This opinion was so general that a friend of mine happening to discuss with one of the Deputies of the Workmen in those Soviets which were being organized just then the conduct of the former Czar, asked if he thought it likely the life of the deposed ruler was in danger. He received this characteristic reply:

"In danger? No. He is not worth a shot."

It is likely that the Empress, if she had been asked her opinion, would have agreed with this judgment. Though she had also thrown up her hands and renounced the game, she would not have given up her rights to the Crown that had been put upon her brow with such pomp and ceremony at Moscow twenty-one years before. She would have fought against the insolence of those who had come to demand it from her. Here I must say that, according to the words of one of the two Deputies sent by the Duma to interview Nicholas II. at Pskow, the prestige of the latter's personality as the anointed Czar of All the Russias was still so great that if he had mustered sufficient energy to throw out of the railway carriage the men audacious enough to claim his abdication, this gesture of Imperial rage would have brought back to him the allegiance of the troops. He was living through a terrible drama, and he was accepting it like a comedy. After having disgraced himself, he was dishonoring by his attitude the misfortunes which had fallen on his country, on his dynasty, and on his race.

CHAPTER XXVI

A CROWN IS LOST

THE Monarchy of the Romanoffs had fallen like a house of cards which crumbles on the ground at the slightest touch. It had been considered one of the strongest, one of the most powerful, in Europe; yet its collapse had come with an amazing promptitude and there had not been found in the whole vast Empire over which it had ruled one single man or woman willing to arrest its downward course toward the abyss into which it finally disappeared. What the tyranny of Nicholas I., the selfishness of Alexander II., and the iron rule of Alexander III. had failed to produce, the weakness, indecision, and incapacity of Nicholas II. had made easy. What a German Princess, Catherine II., had maintained, another German Princess compromised and lost forever.

Without wishing to add to the faults and mistakes of Alexandra Feodorowna, it is nevertheless quite impossible to acquit her of blame in the catastrophe which finally wrecked poor, unfortunate Russia. Without her it is likely that the Crown would have kept some prestige, at least in the eyes of those whose family traditions were linked with the fate of the Monarchy in their country. She destroyed this prestige by the singularity of her conduct, the want of balance of her mind, and her proud, haughty, and totally false conception of the Russian character. She firmly believed that nothing she could do would be criticized and that even those who disliked her, whose number was legion, as she knew very well, would never dare to question her right to do whatever she pleased, or to choose her friends no matter in what circles or among what kind of people.

This woman, whom misfortune associated with the fate of the House of Romanoff at the very time when the latter ought to have had the aid of an intelligent, well-intentioned, and unselfish Princess to help it face the dangers which were threatening it, had never known how to put herself at the level of the persons by whom she found herself surrounded. She lacked not only tact, but also generosity, and she never could hold broad views about anything or about anybody. She was as scathing as she was hasty in her judgments. From the very first day she was raised to the Throne of Russia she abused the privileges which her position conferred upon her, and either through stupidity—or willingly—because of her dislike for the nation whose Crown she wore, she applied herself to wound those whom she ought to have spared and to propitiate persons whom it would have been imperative for her to keep away as far as possible from her person and from that of her husband.

Of course she was in a certain sense a strong character, in so far, at least, as she never would yield to reason or accept any compromise. She had principles of her own, which, however, did not help her to win respect for herself or esteem for her conduct. Without ever allowing herself to be led by impulse, she failed to perceive that in most of her actions she was influenced by superstition of a most foolish kind. The fact that insanity existed in her family may excuse her to a certain point, but should not blind us to faults which might easily have been corrected had she only realized their existence.

She was a blameless wife; about this there cannot be any doubt. But she never loved her husband and she only cared for his position. She was a tender mother, at least to her son, whatever may have been her feelings in regard to her daughters, whom she most unjustly blamed for their sex, if we are to believe all that we have been told on the subject. But she lacked sympathy, which she never could give to others or win for herself. She was a cold, ambitious, stern creature, so convinced of her own perfection that she never could be brought to see good in anything with which she was not connected in some way or other. Her life certainly had tragedy entwined with its course. Perhaps the most cruel blow, until the final catastrophe that wrecked all her hopes, had been her unfortunate affection for the dashing officer, Colonel Orloff, who had died to save her honor and good name, whose post-mortem influence had been so cleverly made use of by unscrupulous adventurers in order to win her confidence. Alexandra had always at heart despised the weak man to whom she was married, but she had loved the high position which, thanks to her union with him, she had acquired; she would have liked to remain alone in control of it and to revenge her supposed wrongs at the hands of the Russian nation, by delivering it into the power of that German Fatherland of hers to which she had always remained attached. Her desire for peace was sincere (at least we must hope so), and everything we know about her and about her conduct during that momentous time when she kept working toward its conclusion points to the truth of this supposition. It had all along been a terrible trial for her to find the land of her birth at war with that of her adoption, and to this initial agony was added the superstitious terror which Raspoutine had inspired in her, thanks to the hypnotic practices in which he had induced her to participate—terror which ended by completely wrecking her already badly balanced mind.

But the supreme misfortune of the last Empress of Russia, a misfortune for which she was not responsible, was the fact of her having been married to a being who was too weak to lead her, too selfish to understand her, too cruelly inclined to sympathize with her; who at the same time did not acquire sufficient authority over her to inspire her with respect for his individuality as a man and for his position as a Sovereign. Had she been the wife of Alexander III., it is likely that she would have turned out entirely another woman from the one which she ultimately became; on the other hand, had Nicholas II. had for Consort a person different from the one to whom destiny had linked him, it is also probable that he would have contrived to avoid some of the mistakes into which he fell. He might have shown himself more plucky and more human in the different moments of crisis which made his reign such a sad and such an unfortunate one.

One of the most tragical things with which a student of history finds himself confronted when he analyzes any of the great catastrophes that come to change the fate of nations is the total insufficiency of the people who have to meet them or to handle them. There is no more pitiful spectacle than the vacillations of Louis XVI. during the first days of the great Revolution which sent him to the scaffold. Witness the want of character of the miserable Czar who is meditating at present in Tobolsk over the misfortunes that have landed him into exile; it is another of those sights one should have liked to see spared to posterity. During the twenty-two years he occupied the Russian Throne Nicholas II. constantly opposed himself to the wishes of his people, even the most reasonable ones, when he thought that they implied any diminution of his personal prerogatives or power. He sent hundreds of thousands of innocent people to the gallows or to horrible Siberian prisons under the slightest of pretexts. He had no hesitation at spilling the blood of his subjects either on the battle-field or on the scaffold. He allowed the detestable police system, which became, under his rule, stronger than it had ever been before, to interfere with private liberty and private opinions to an extent that had never been witnessed in his country even in the times of Nicholas I. or of Paul. While he reigned no one felt secure in his home or could go to bed with the consciousness that he would not be wakened in the middle of the night by an army of police agents come to search his drawers, or to arrest him under the most futile of pretexts or simply because he had refused to pay a bribe. And yet that man in whose name the most terrible injustices had been committed, who did not admit any resistance to his will, who believed in his unlimited power over one hundred and eighty millions of human beings—that man did not find sufficient courage to resist the only demand, among the many which were addressed to him during the course of his nefarious reign, that he ought never to have granted; and without one single thought of the future of his country or of his son he gave up without a murmur the Crown of which he was the bearer, when two determined men came to claim it from him, and he did so without even noticing that they were far more awed by the solemnity of the scene in which they found themselves unwilling actors than he was himself.

There never was a Throne relinquished with less dignity, there never was an act of abdication accomplished with less consciousness of the importance of its meaning. When one recapitulates all the details of the drama which was performed at Pskow, one can, when one is a Russian, feel but one passionate regret—that no one was found by the side of the last crowned Romanoff to drive a knife into his heart or put a bullet through his brain, and thus spare this haughty dynasty the shame of having been dragged into the gutter by its Head.

It is scarcely to be doubted that if Nicholas II. had only given more thought to the importance of the act he was invited to perform he might at least have saved his dynasty, if not himself. His brother, the Grand-Duke Michael, who could easily renounce the Crown for himself, would hardly have been able to refuse the Regency on behalf of his little nephew. A man with the slightest political knowledge would have put the interests of his country before his own selfish feelings of paternal affection, and the Czar ought to have abdicated in favor of his son, and not have put forward this stupid pretext of lacking the courage to part from him. This very remark proves how little he understood the situation in which he found himself. It also shows us how utterly helpless he was when confronted by any difficulties of an overpowering and potential character. When one considers his whole conduct during those eventful hours when he lost not only his own, but his posterity's, Crown, it is impossible not to wonder as to whether or not there was any truth in the rumor that the Empress had been giving him drugs of some kind with the purpose of annihilating his will. It seems almost incredible that any man should have so quietly and so spontaneously lent a hand to his own degradation.

It is to be doubted, also, whether he regretted what he had done. Certainly he never imagined to what it would lead him. The idea that his people would have the courage to make him a prisoner does not seem to have crossed his mind, any more than did the fact that, once he had lost his position, he had become not only a useless, but an embarrassing factor in Russian politics. He went back to Mohilew, to the headquarters of that army of which he had been the Commander-in-chief as well as the Sovereign, quite naturally and in the same quiet manner he might have done in the days gone by. He did not even seem to yearn after his wife and children, and never once did he suggest the advisability of returning to Tsarskoye Selo. Of all the people assembled around him he appeared the most unconcerned. This indifference lasted even when he found himself faced with captivity and when the former Head of his Staff, General Aléxieieff, came to acquaint him with the decision of the Provisional Government to arrest him.

His wife, left alone in the Palace where she had spent so many happy days, did not perhaps share his indifference; she certainly displayed the same apathy. Alexandra Feodorowna, from the moment that she saw her schemes of personal grandeur frustrated, gave up the game; she gave it up with more dignity than her husband had ever shown—this much must be conceded to her. She never flinched before the insults that were poured down upon her; she never gave a sign that she was moved to anything else but disdain when General Korniloff read to her the orders of the Government in regard to her person, and acquainted her with the fact that she was a prisoner. She declared to the few people left with her that she considered herself only as a Sister of Charity in attendance on her sick children. The Empress had disappeared, outwardly at least, and perhaps it was just as well that she accepted the situation in this way, rather than attempt a useless resistance, which could only have added to her unpopularity.

But still the fact remained that the whole Russian Revolution had been conducted after the style of a comic opera of Offenbach. No one at first had recognized its serious character. No one had seemed to realize that it constituted the most portentous event of the last hundred years or so. Those who had carried it out had done it on the spur of the moment, without thinking of what would follow; and the Monarch who had bowed his head under its decrees also had not suspected that a morrow was there, waiting for the results of what was being done to-day. The historical stick that had been wielded by Peter the Great had been transformed into the ridiculous sword of the Grand Duchess of Gerolstein.

CHAPTER XXVII

A PRISONER AFTER HAVING BEEN A QUEEN

A NEW life began for Alexandra Feodorowna. Until that fatal day when she was taken into captivity her existence had been one of ease and luxury. She had been the Empress of All the Russias, being revered by some as almost a divinity, the absolute mistress of all her surroundings, with servants in attendance on her, eager to execute any commands it might please her to lay upon them. She had not a wish which was not instantly gratified; the misfortunes that had assailed her (I am not speaking now of those that fell upon Russia) had always left her indifferent; they had existed more in her imagination than in reality. Suddenly without warning and, what was even worse, at the very moment when she had expected to reach even loftier heights than the one upon which she was placed, she had been hurled down into an abyss of sorrow, of misery, and of pain such as she had never imagined she could ever know. She was no longer a Sovereign; her courtiers, servants, attendants, had all vanished with the exception of a very few, and those she had never cared for much, in the days of her prosperity. Her children were sick and she could not even obtain for them a doctor's help. Her friends had fled or were in prison; her Crown had been wrested from her; she was a prisoner, deprived of the means of communicating with her own people and relatives; the guards who surrounded her Palace were no longer placed there to protect her safety; they were intrusted with another mission, that of watching over every one of her movements and of preventing her from getting any news from the outside world. Instead of crowds gathered to cheer her, she saw assembled under her windows an angry multitude asking for her blood and calling out to her that she ought to be punished as a traitor. She had no friends, no money, no influence any longer. The dream had come to an end, and she found herself facing stern reality, a reality against which it was useless to struggle.

Her husband came back to her, a prisoner, likewise, but with perhaps less consciousness of the horror of their position than she had. They had to settle down to a new life entirely different from the previous one—a life of idleness, of inaction; an existence which made them realize with every step they took the awful change that had overtaken them. When they wished to go out they had to ask permission to do so from an officer who often refused it out of pure malice. They had to pass before sentinels who no longer presented arms to them, who only sneered in their faces as they saw them hurry through a room or a corridor, anxious to escape insult or outrage. No one was allowed to come near them. They were condemned to a solitude in which they were continually reminded of the days gone by forever.

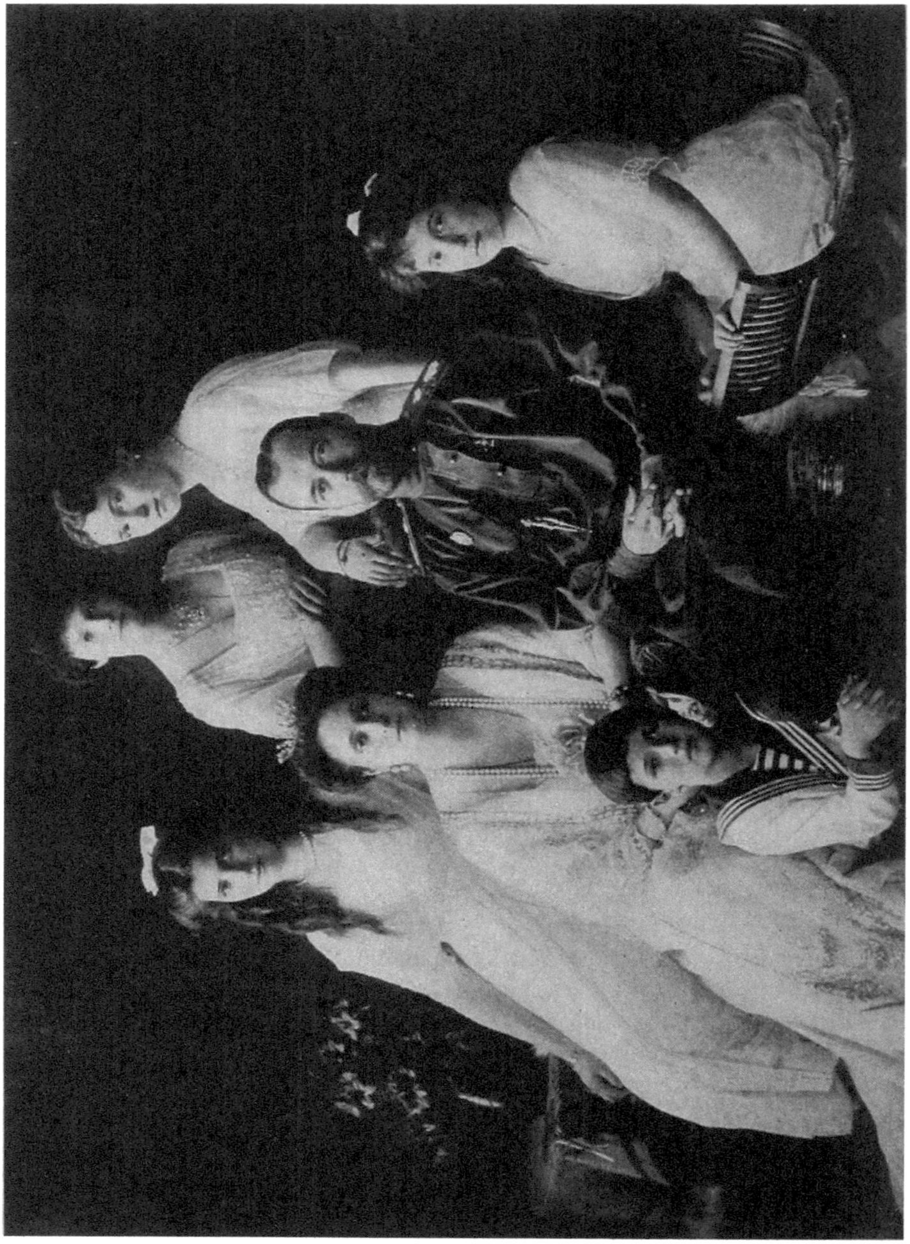

The Royal Family

Seated, from left to right: The Grand-Duchess Marie; the Czarina, with the little Grand-Duke Alexis at her knee; the Czar; the Grand-Duchess Anastasia, the youngest of the four girls. Standing, from left to right: The Grand-Duchess Tatiana, and the Grand-Duchess Olga immediately behind her father.

A few faithful attendants had been left them, it is true, but these last friends were just as badly off as themselves, and could do but very little to alleviate the miseries of a position which was an illustration of the famous verses of Dante, that there is nothing more dreadful during days of misery than to remember the past joyful ones. Even religion, which for such a long period of years had consoled the Empress in many sad and troubled hours, had ceased to be a comfort to her; divine service, during which her name and that of her husband were carefully omitted from the liturgy, was only one new source of torment for her. It seemed to her as if the Church as well as the Russian nation repulsed her and treated her as a pariah and an outcast. Another woman, with higher, loftier views, would have looked with more philosophy on these small sides in a great tragedy, might perhaps even have failed to notice them. But for Alexandra Feodorowna they constituted something far more tangible and real than the fact that the House of Romanoff had lost its Throne.

She would most probably have wished to discuss with the Czar all the events which had brought about the catastrophe, but even this comfort was denied to her. The Provisional Government had issued orders that husband and wife should not be permitted to communicate with or see each other, except in presence of witnesses. Some people have said that this was an unnecessary cruelty, but it seems that there was some reason for this decision. A strong party at that time was clamoring for repressive measures in regard to the ex-Empress. Papers had been found in which her negotiations with the Kaiser had been revealed, and the question of bringing her to trial had been seriously discussed. But no one wished to see the former Czar mixed up with this business, as it was generally felt it would be a great political mistake to make a martyr out of him.

There was, however, ground to fear that if he were permitted to speak with his wife alone, she would contrive in some way or other to entangle him in her personal intrigues. This Mr. Miliukoff, then Minister for Foreign Affairs, wished to avoid, for reasons of a general political order, and Mr. Kerensky for other ones of a purely personal character. It seems that this leader of the Socialist party in the Duma had, before events had transformed him into a Minister, spoken also with certain agents of the Kaiser who had contrived to remain in the Russian capital. Nicholas II. had friends who, knowing this fact, warned the radical chief that if any harm was done to the former Sovereign his own participation in eventual peace negotiations with the enemy would be exposed. Can one imagine that when Nicholas was told of this fact he only blamed those who had thus attempted to save him, saying that he did not like blackmail of any kind, even when it was performed for his advantage? That man who had been one of the most important political factors of his time was not even shrewd enough to see that it was only politics which could save his life after they had dispossessed him of his Throne.

The Provisional Government, so long as decent men composed it, would have been willing to spare any unnecessary humiliations to the former Czar and his family. Unfortunately, the military men who had been put in charge of the Palace of Tsarskoye Selo and of its inhabitants did not share this opinion, and there is no doubt but that the deposed Monarch was subjected to insult, as well as to all kinds of small and petty annoyances calculated to make him feel bitterly the change in his position. I do not believe personally in the tales which were put into circulation as to his having been hustled about by the soldiers on guard at the castle the day he had returned there a State prisoner from Mohilew, a few short weeks after he had left it a powerful Sovereign. For one thing, his devoted aide-de-camp, Prince Dolgoroukoff, was with him, and he would most certainly have interfered had any violence been used in regard to his master. But the unfortunate Nicholas was made in other ways to drink the cup of humiliation to the dregs. The troops were told not to salute him; the sentries were forbidden to present arms to him; he was addressed as Colonel Romanoff by his jailers; his letters were opened and his expenses controlled in a searching, insulting manner which must have been terribly bitter for him to bear. Every kind of newspaper containing insults addressed to him or to the Empress were sent to him or put in his way. When he went out in the park he was often accosted by people who upbraided him for all the misfortunes that had fallen upon Russia, for which they made him responsible. I do not mention insignificant daily worries, such as the shutting off of the electric light, or of the water-pipes, so that the unfortunate Imperial Family was left without baths, and other small unpleasantnesses of the same kind. These would perhaps not have been noticed if the other ones had not been there to remind the once powerful Czar of All the Russias that he was at the mercy of the subjects whose rights he had not respected and whose cries for freedom he had quenched in blood.

But Nicholas, in the midst of all these miseries, preserved the same impassibility he had displayed when the news of the disasters of Mukden and Tsu Shima had been brought to him, or when he had heard that Warsaw and the long line of fortresses that had defended the Russian frontier on the Niemen and the Vistula had fallen into German hands. He accepted everything with stoicism; he expressed no surprise at the blows which were being hurled at his head. He simply remained indifferent, perhaps because he was too much of a fatalist to rebel, but most probably because he had not yet grasped the real significance of all that was happening to him.

The Empress was not so resigned, in spite of her apparent apathy. She had more reasons to fear for her personal safety than her husband, and she knew very well that in case of a rising of the anarchists in Petrograd she would be the first victim they would claim. This dread led her into another of the mistakes which she was continually perpetrating, the mistake of trying to call to her rescue her German cousin.

According to people whom I have reason to believe exceptionally well informed, she caused certain information to be carried to the Kaiser. In return for this she implored him to try and save her, together with her children. Of course this became known to the Provisional Government, but the latter wished to spare her, partly because it feared that if her new misdeeds were published nothing could save her from the wrath of the public, and it did not wish the Revolution to be dishonored by the murder of a defenseless woman, whatever that woman might have done. But the question of the transfer of Nicholas II. and of his family to a place where he could be guarded more closely than at Tsarskoye Selo was discussed seriously. It is likely that this would have been executed already during the first six weeks which followed upon his abdication if other things had not interfered, and if in rapid succession the men who had taken up the task he had been unable to fulfil had not in their turn disappeared one after the other, making room for Ministers more advanced in their opinions and more devoid of scruples as to the punishment which they believed ought to be inflicted on the former Emperor.

Alexandra Feodorowna had been subjected to a strict examination of her political activity by the military authorities in charge of the district of Petrograd, and particularly by General Korniloff, who had a personal grudge against her and who did not spare her in the scathing reproaches which he addressed to her. But nothing could shake the equanimity of the haughty Czarina. She sneered at the General, she scorned his threats, and proudly declared to him that she would not reply to any of his questions, as she did not recognize his right to address them to her. While her husband showed no sign of impatience under the affronts which were showered down upon him (on the contrary, he exhibited absolute submission to the will of those who had taken him captive), the Empress remembered the position which she had occupied a few days before, and simply smiled at her persecutors with a disdain that had certainly something exasperating about it if one considers the intellectual and moral standard of the people to whom this proof of her contempt was addressed.

Alexandra refused to show that she suffered from the change that had taken place in her position, while her husband hardly knew whether he was suffering from it or not. There lay the difference in their two characters and in their way of meeting the catastrophe which had changed their whole lives and destinies.

There came, however, a day when the composure of the Consort of Nicholas II. failed, when she at last gave way to despair. It was during the afternoon when her friend and the confidante of all her thoughts, Anna Wyrubewa, was taken away from her, and carried off to the fortress of SS. Peter and Paul in Petrograd. Until that day the Empress had not felt quite alone in her misery. There was at least near her one person with whom she could speak about all those dear dead ones whose memory she either cherished or worshiped. So long as that friend was there the miserable Empress could talk about Orloff, Raspoutine, and the prayer-meetings during which the latter evoked for her the spirit of the former. When Anna was taken away from her this last consolation came also to an end. Henceforward the solitude of Alexandra Feodorowna was to be complete; and nothing was left to her except her eyes to weep, and her memory to remind her of those whom she had loved and lost. The horrors which were to follow, the Siberian exile whither she was to be sent, were to leave her unmoved. She had inwardly died in that terrible hour when the last friend and the sharer of all the secrets of her life had been snatched away from her arms.

CHAPTER XXVIII

THE EXILE

THESE days in Tsarskoye Selo which seemed so hard to bear were Paradise compared with what awaited the previous masters of this Imperial place.

Soon there came one August morning when a man who a few months before had been known only as one of the leaders of that Socialist party which the Government of Nicholas II. had taken such trouble to suppress, and whom the tide of events had transformed into one of the Ministers of the new Russian Republic, Alexander Feodorovitch Kerensky, entered, uncalled for and unannounced, into the private apartments of the former Czar, and acquainted him with the new decision to which the Government of the day had come in regard to his person and to the fate of his family. How he did it, how he mustered the courage to inform the fallen Monarch that he was about to be exiled to that distant Siberia, where so many people had been sent during his reign and had gone cursing his name, no one knows. None of the actors in this scene ever revealed its details.

It is probable, however, that Kerensky had experienced far more emotion in signifying to the deposed Sovereign the horrible punishment to which he had been condemned than the latter had displayed when receiving the terrible news, the nature of which must have completely bewildered him. Of all the things he had expected, this was certainly the last. The possibility of a public trial, in imitation of the one of Louis XVI. in France, had been discussed between the Emperor and the Empress, and they had in a certain sense both schooled themselves for such a supreme ordeal. But exile in cold, bleak Siberia, in that land of mystery and of crime, of heroic deeds and ignoble deaths—this solution of the difficulties of a position which was daily growing more threatening had never presented itself to the mind of the last Russian Autocrat. Tobolsk, too! This dreariest spot in a dreary country; this accursed place from which all those who could do so fled away with alacrity! What could have been more awful than to have chosen it as the future residence of a Monarch who, if all was well considered, had by his own act rendered himself impossible as a ruler in the future? No political necessity required his being sent so far and there were many other places where he might have been just as safe, and not quite so unhappy, as in that small Siberian town. Can one wonder if despair took hold of the souls of the unhappy Czar and of his wife? Can one wonder if he exclaimed that he would have preferred to die rather than have to meet such an atrocious fate?

There were his children, too; his innocent children, who had done no harm and who were to share this miserable destiny to which he was condemned. Kerensky had told him that the young Grand Duchesses and their brother would be left free to follow their parents in that distant land whither they were to depart, or to remain in Russia if they preferred. But this was almost adding insult to an abominable injury, because the children could hardly do anything else than decide to accompany their father and mother. Verily nothing was to be spared to Nicholas II., not even the knowledge that his daughters and his idolized boy were about to be exposed to hardships which it was hardly likely they could survive.

Nevertheless, he took the news bravely, and neither he nor Alexandra Feodorowna murmured. The latter is credited with having remarked that the new Government had evidently wanted to please her by sending them to a place that could only be dear to her on account of its associations with Raspoutine, who had been born there. Whether this is exact or not I will not undertake to say. What is true, however, is that she left with dry eyes the place where she had spent so many happy years, and that not even during the religious service, which was celebrated in the private chapel of the Palace, when the blessings of Heaven were invoked in favor of people about to start on a long journey, did she shed a tear. All the other assistants, including her daughters, sobbed passionately and bitterly the whole time that it lasted.

Though the hour of the departure of Nicholas had been kept as secret as possible, the whole town of Tsarskoye Selo knew that he was about to leave it forever. The population for once was awed before the immensity of the disaster. One was used in Russia to people being sent to Siberia; one had seen a Menschikoff, a Biren, a Dolgorouky, and more recently a Prince Troubetskoy, and a Mourawieff-Apostol, start on this dreaded journey whence so few ever returned. But here was something different. Here was a Romanoff about to go there where his ancestors and himself had deported so many, so many, entirely innocent people. Here was the dreaded Sovereign, whose name had been for such a long time mentioned only with reverence and with fear, exiled like one of those persons whom he had sent to Siberia with a mere stroke of his pen. Here was Nicholas II., formerly Emperor and Autocrat of All the Russias, here was the mighty Czar who had been crowned at Moscow, reduced to the condition of a common criminal by the subjects whose rights he had violated, whose consciences he had trampled upon, whose liberty he had taken away, and whose lives he had in so many instances tried to destroy. Truly the sight was appalling, and there were but few among those who in the early twilight of a summer morning looked at that mournful train which was carrying away toward the distant north so much dead grandeur and such awful misfortune, there were but few who did not realize that they were witnessing something more tragic and more solemn even than a funeral, that they were looking upon the end of a great chapter in Russian history, and that it was not only a Czar who lay buried under all these ruins, but also something of the past glories of the country.

They had been, after all, together with the future of the Romanoff dynasty, a great race that had produced great men and they deserved to have, as their last crowned descendant, some one better than Nicholas II. had proved to be. They had often been cruel, more frequently even unjust; they had never respected what the world is used to venerate and to esteem; they had shown themselves hard in regard to their subjects; but they had made out of dark, ignorant Russia an immense Empire on which even more immense hopes had been built. They had exercised on several occasions a restraining influence over the exaggerations of half-educated and half-instructed men with all the instincts of the savage and but few of the qualities of the civilized being. They had led their people through danger, through war, through many momentous days of rejoicing as well as of anguish. They had been a part of the Russian nation, and with their disgrace and fall something in that nation, too, had been dishonored and had perished.

With the personal failure of Nicholas II. this book has nothing to do. From the very first day that he had ascended the Throne of Russia it had been evident to any person gifted with the talent of observation that his reign was bound to end in disaster and in ruin; that all the work performed by his late father, who, after all, when things are well considered, had been a great man and a wise Sovereign, would very soon be destroyed by his want of character and of principle and by his abominable selfishness. People, however, had hoped that during the years supreme power remained concentrated in his hands at least blood would not flow. No one's imagination had conceived the horrors of Mukden and of Tsu Shima, nor the massacres which took place at Tannenberg and in the Polish plains. No one had suspected that the rivers would be dyed red while he went on living unconscious and unconcerned about all the misery which would remain forever associated with his name. When destiny was at last fulfilled in regard to him, it was discovered that it had also been fulfilled in regard to Russia, and this was what the country could not bring itself to forgive him; this is what his ancestors also would not have pardoned him had they been able to arise out of their graves, and to

> Rend the gold brocade
> Whereof their shroud was made[1]

in horror at all the evil perpetrated by their unworthy descendant.

Yes, in the past they had been a strong race, these Romanoffs, about whom no one thinks any longer to-day in the vast realm that owned them once as its masters and lords. But it would be useless to deny that crimes without number were committed by them and that injustice flourished during the centuries when they could dispose absolutely of the fate of millions and millions of human creatures whom they killed and tortured at their will and according to their fancies. Perhaps it was a just punishment for the ruthless cruelty of some of them that the glories of their race came to an end and perished, together with all the traditions that had surrounded them for such a long time, because of the follies, sins, mistakes, blunderings, iniquities, and indecisions of a weak, characterless, and half-witted man and of a superstitious, intriguing, and half-demented woman.

THE END.

[1] Longfellow, "The White Czar."

9 789361 384059

Printed by Libri Plureos GmbH in Hamburg,
Germany